Par Successfully with American Firms

HOW TO WORK EFFECTIVELY WITH
U.S. COMPANIES AND BUSINESSPEOPLE

Ali Shami
Steven Howard

Caliente Press

Partnering Successfully with American Firms
How to Work Effectively with U.S. Companies and Businesspeople

Published by:
Caliente Press
1775 E Palm Canyon Drive, Suite 110-198
Palm Springs, CA 92264
www.CalientePress.com
Email: steven@CalientePress.com

Cover Design: Héctor Castañeda

ENDORSEMENTS AND PRAISE

In today's globally interconnected environment, where cultural diversity abounds, understanding one's business partners is paramount for organizations to navigate international and corporate boundaries effectively.

Drawing from my extensive 33-year tenure at an American institution in Lebanon, I value authors who acknowledge the importance of recognizing the distinct "Americanized" business traits crucial when collaborating with American organizations. Bridging cultural disparities demands cultural agility—genuinely appreciating and adapting to diverse cultural norms.

I wholeheartedly endorse the book's assertion that true understanding of meaning, beliefs, history, traditions, norms, and values necessitates courageously venturing beyond one's comfort zone into the vast expanse of cultural dimensions.

This manuscript delves into a timely and pertinent subject within the business landscape, offering invaluable insights into partnering with American corporations. The book's adept use of examples and best practices elucidates its concepts effectively.

It is a comprehensive resource for those seeking to grasp the foundational elements underpinning successful partnerships with American firms.

This book covers topics ranging from resilience and agility to American corporate culture, negotiation strategies, cultural awareness, communication proficiency, emotional intelligence, and comprehension of the intricate US legal system at both state and federal levels. It equips readers with a robust toolkit for navigating cross-cultural collaborations.

The authors' combined wealth of over 70 years of professional experience shines through, enabling them to comprehensively address the multifaceted dimensions outlined in the book's objectives with exceptional clarity and insight.

H.E. Professor Hassan B. Diab
Prime Minister (2020-21) of Lebanon

I think this book is not just about global ideas for Leaders and Executives but also a very practical guide, full of hands-on useful tips for the working level of companies wanting to succeed with US corporations!

It reminds us that working together is all about human factors, and those are all about managing the little details of cultural differences — like art as written!

Thomas Sonigo
VP Aircraft Modification
Air France

Partnering Successfully with American Firms by Steven Howard and Ali Shami is an indispensable guide for international executives, entrepreneurs, and business educators engaged in global commerce.

This book delves deep into the complexities of the U.S. business environment, offering a clear roadmap for navigating cultural differences and forging lasting partnerships. Its practical insights into cross-cultural negotiations and strategic business practices make it an essential resource for all professionals aiming to excel in the interconnected global market.

Miguel Angel Iglesias Bueno
Director
Axion Mexico

Ali and Steven have created a business practices book that should be kept in the back pocket of anyone wanting to fully understand the American way of doing successful business in a quickly changing world through people, business strategy, and ethics. It's an essential resource to ensure you get a full understanding of and insight into American culture and shared values. The book highlights the changes to how we do business and how quickly these changes to business plans are becoming in order to stay ahead in the international and the globally changing playing fields of business.

From a British business point of view, and now having worked with you and your team/s directly for almost six years, it was essential that both companies (which had a gap of a decade since working closely together), through these selected individuals, that would have to develop into a team as working as a team from the day 1 in order to achieve the best delivery outcomes and ensured reputations were not compromised.

The experience, oversight, and influence you created and the positive atmosphere allowed the development of the delivery team's ability to break down barriers, made the essentials of trust, shared goals, and behaviors helped with the team dynamics and the creation of a successful team.

It's not by accident that this team gelled as quickly as it did, and that was down to Ali's comprehensive depth of experience and knowledge using his extensive leadership and business acumen, plus his "human touch" knowledge and his keen listening skills. Utilizing these skills to work with a multicultural international group of airline customers, each with differing needs and wants and "red Lines." He balanced that with his own company deliverables and costs to ensure his customers also succeeded. This book opens up all of this to aid these initial relationship-building essentials critical to establishing a successful business/partnership in the USA.

Glen MacDonald
Former Long-Haul Fleet Chief
British Airways

I wholeheartedly recommend reading *Partnering Successfully with American Firms*. It is an indispensable resource and tool for international businesspeople to be used as a practical guide to respond proactively and swiftly to the ever-changing and dynamic global business environment. Through insightful analysis and practical experiences, the authors illuminate the importance of recognizing and respecting cultural differences in international business partnerships while keeping the big picture in mind that "we are all part of one humanity and that our similarities outweigh our differences."

The authors also explicitly emphasize that a successful international businessperson equipped with cross-cultural understanding "will also help make the world a more peaceful, kinder, and compassionate for our children and grandchildren to inherit."

Yonas Yeshanow
Former Director of Engineering and Maintenace
Ethiopian Airlines

As a UK citizen, this book is an absolute joy to read about doing business the right way with an American firm. It is full of straightforward and honest thinking, tips, and know-how. It is a go-to book for anyone thinking or doing business with an American organization.

Andrew Elliman
Head of European Business Development
AGS Worldwide
London

Contents

Dedication

We Dedicate This Book To:

Edwin B. Cohen
Host of Global TV Talkshow

A master at bringing people
across the world
to discuss important business topics.

And who brought us together.

Thank you for all your support for us,
individually and collectively.

Introduction

Many, perhaps even most, American business leaders expect their international counterparts to be fluent in the American business culture. At the same time, international executives value themselves as equal partners and expect American leaders to understand and appreciate their respective national business cultures.

Closing this gap often boils down to answering the following question by both American and international executives: Do you want to be Right or Rich?

Why not both? Especially in today's continuously growing and interconnected global economies.

Bookstores (and Amazon) are stacked with books on how Americans can conduct business outside the U.S. The Internet contains thousands of articles and advice on building trust and communicating with other cultures. On the other hand, the results are practically nil when searching for how to partner or do business with Americans. Thus, this book becomes a great resource for foreign businesses looking to establish partnerships with American businesses and learn how to be reliable, desired, and sought-after suppliers, partners, and customers.

Maybe the perception is that Hollywood is doing all the training needed for the world to understand Americans and the American business culture. However, while Hollywood does a good job of introducing American culture and business practices to the rest of the world in an entertaining way, it unfortunately projects a shallow perspective of American business ethos, standards, and values. To successfully partner or deal with American businesses, it is important to understand and appreciate the nuances, subtleties, and idiosyncrasies of how Americans do business at home and globally. Those who do so will benefit by taking their relationships with American firms to much higher levels.

However, the genuine interest in connecting with other cultures on intellectual and emotional levels is more important as long as one stays within what is expected from an outsider of the culture!

Does this recommendation apply to international companies planning to partner with American firms? Absolutely!

The authors of this book believe that every nation on earth appreciates those who respect other cultures. The pithy saying "when in Rome" applies to America as well. This is especially important, considering American businesses have enjoyed success for decades, domestically and internationally. To be successful, emulate the successful!

Unfortunately, many American business leaders show dissatisfaction with businesspeople from other cultures who do not adopt and subscribe to the American business culture. Equally unfortunate, they believe the American way of doing business is the only viable global business culture.

In some ways, this can be expected. After all, American businesses have been leading the world's economic growth for decades. During this span, numerous international companies understood that adopting American business methodologies and practices increased their chances of succeeding. Those who did usually enjoyed long-lasting business partnerships with American and Western firms.

Adapting to other cultures while doing business with them does not mean completely letting go of your cultural values. It just provides the opportunity to get closer to the minds and hearts of people who grew up in other cultures and work in those cultures.

One of the biggest mistakes international companies make when they embark on joint ventures with American companies is not realizing how their employees may struggle to deal with other cultures. Instead, they base their decision to partner together on how well their respective CEOs work together and communicate with their American opposite number.

Two CEOS from different cultures and companies discussing the possibility of partnering may not foresee any challenges with the partnership since they both may have so much in common (social status, schooling, global business experience, etc.). Their cultural and business ideology differences are narrow in scope and scale.

The cultural gap problem gets amplified when managers and workers from both companies start working together. This is where most of the cross-cultural issues lead to unsuccessful outcomes. Business leaders and book authors have focused on creating trust, connecting with different cultures, and assisting Americans to conduct successful business transactions abroad. The truth is that there are very few publications available with advice for non-Americans on forming partnerships with Americans.

Hence the reason for this book. We aim to help you successfully work with American firms, executives, leaders, and managers – whether you sell to, partner with, or buy from American businesses.

Why should you take our advice? Because we are both road-tested in the international business arena. We know what works and what doesn't. We know what creates angst, anger, friction, and hurdles between American businesspeople and their counterparts across the globe despite the best intentions of all parties. Most importantly, we know how to prevent these problems from escalating and causing less-than-optimal outcomes.

One of the authors (Ali) was born in Lebanon and migrated to the United States at the age of 20. In his long and successful career as a senior manager at The Boeing Company, he was at the forefront of helping the aircraft manufacturer negotiate deals and sell products and services in numerous countries and markets. He led teams in Operations, Customer Service, Customer Engineering, Sales & Marketing, Manufacturing, Product Development, Supplier Management, and Global Engineering. He also had international assignments in Korea, Italy, and England.

Though born and raised in America, the other author (Steven) has spent over 35 years living outside the U.S., working in senior executive positions in marketing, advertising, sales management, and leadership development. His corporate career included stints at Texas Instruments, TIME Magazine, BBDO Advertising, and Citibank. In addition to the U.S. states of California, Nevada, and Texas, he has lived in Singapore, Australia, and Mexico.

Despite their cultural differences and expatriate lives, both authors have similar perspectives on how best to hurdle cultural chasms successfully, professionally and personally. We will share our respective stories and experiences to move you through the learning curve of doing business with American firms faster. And help you avoid the pitfalls and mistakes we see too many smart, but inexperienced, people make trying to navigate American business culture.

Awareness of the cultural dimensions and behaviors Americans typically adhere to wholeheartedly is the foundation for success. As is learning how to gain the trust of your American partners. We will explain these cultural dimensions and behaviors to help you become a valued, long-term business partner for American business leaders and their firms.

Lastly, we believe that as more people work and partner with others outside their core cultures, a greater portion of the world's population will understand that we are all part of one humanity and that our similarities outweigh our differences. By implementing the tips and techniques in *Partnering Successfully With American Firms,* not only will you become a more successful international businessperson, you will also help make the world a more peaceful, kinder, and compassionate world for our children and grandchildren to inherit. And for that, we thank you.

We wish you continued success on your journey. We are each available to help you overcome any specific challenges or hurdles you face.

Best wishes for continued success,
Ali Shami (Seattle)
Steven Howard (Mexico City)
June 2024

Terminology

Before diving into and highlighting the differences in cultural dimensions between Americans and the rest of the world, it is important to define the terms we use in this book as follows:

International leaders or companies – Companies not based in the United States and leaders not born or educated in the U.S.

American leaders and companies – U.S.-based companies operating nationally, regionally, or globally with a predominantly American business culture and mindset and usually led by American-born executives.

National Cultures and Corporate Cultures – A corporate culture in a particular country is similar to that of siblings in a family. Families undoubtedly share many traits and customs, but there are always opportunities for individualism and distinctive self-expression.

American businesses are run by people who typically follow the American culture in which they were raised. The employees of American firms, no matter where they are working or interacting, are thus impacted and influenced by inculcated American social and business cultures. However, they also operate according to their own personalities and the social cultures in which they were raised and educated.

The same applies to all multinational companies. The national cultures of their origins strongly influence their business practices, ethics, and values.

CHAPTER 1

Opportunities in a Changing World

In a world preoccupied with global economic uncertainty, wars, continuing supply chain issues, record inflation, rising interest rates, massive layoffs, and people quitting organizations in previously unheard numbers, today's business environment is — at best — confusing, incoherent, and unpredictable. Yet, despite the enormous importance of these issues, we believe there is a more important issue facing global business leaders and the future successes of their organizations.

Why? Because these global issues are temporary and have been emerging for centuries. By the time you read this book, some may be resolved, and others (interest rates, inflation, large-scale layoffs) may be headed in different directions than at the time of this writing. Others may be moderated or escalated in scope (the Great Resignation and Quiet Quitting trends could go in either direction).

On the other hand, the major issue impacting global businesses is systemic. It is not likely to change drastically in our lifetime. Fortunately, however, it can be managed successfully on an individual and organizational basis.

What is the main issue? Organizations and individuals generally cannot cross the national and corporate barriers impeding effective and successful partnerships. This problem is a two-way street: non-American firms and their employees also need help understanding how to work with American firms and vice versa.

This is not to say that all organizations and individuals have failed to figure this out. Yet, from our experiences and observations as two professionals working and living in the international business arena for a combined 70+ years, true successes are a rarity and often for shorter tenures than originally conceived.

We frequently witness cooperative agreements negotiated by senior executives full of hope, pride, and optimism. These idyllic arrangements are too often short-circuited by the inability of their respective teams to understand one another, communicate clearly and effectively, implement shared goals, and overcome the intrinsic barriers and hurdles to cross-cultural and cross-border cooperation.

This problem has been exacerbated by the increasing activity of small and medium-sized businesses wanting to do business outside their home countries. Unfortunately, they do not have the financial or knowledge resources to train their employees in multicultural awareness and skills. Thus, the successful players in the international arena tend to be the big boys – the larger organizations and companies that can afford to invest in training and have the financial resources to weather the financial burdens when things do not go according to plan.

Despite these challenges, there are opportunities galore for companies and individuals seeking to grow their businesses or operations by working with or partnering with American firms. So do not despair. Utilizing the information, tips, and techniques in *Partnering Successfully With American Firms* will propel you to greater success, more fruitful working relationships, and fewer bumps along the way.

Why the focus on working and partnering with American firms? Quite frankly, that is the area of our experience and expertise. We are not in a position to advise how to partner with Chinese, Indian, Latin American, African, or European firms. However, the core principles in this book will also provide excellent first steps for engaging with non-American firms.

The other reasons for doing business with American firms are highlighted in the next section.

Why Do Business with American Firms?

It is really quite simple. The United States remains the big gorilla in the global marketplace. Yes, China and India are growing rapidly. So is Mexico, partly due to the nearshoring opportunities for manufacturers selling into the U.S. and Canada. Other nations are also starting to rebound from the economic fallout of the Covid-19 pandemic. But the U.S. remains the big behemoth. As the old saying goes, *"When the U.S. sneezes, other countries catch a cold."*

Another strong point in favor of doing business with American firms is that the U.S. has a business-favorable and entrenched legal system at both the state and federal levels. This reduces contract compliance risk compared to countries without a robust and comprehensible legal structure.

Additionally, in the U.S., you have readily available access to capital markets (both private and public), technology, economic prowess, and privately owned businesses. In other countries, you must deal with government-owned or government-linked companies (particularly in China, Singapore, and Malaysia) or with only a handful of mega-conglomerates (such as in India, Thailand, and Japan). So, your options are greater and more legally protected in the United States.

This, of course, is not an either/or situation. You can do business and partner with companies and organizations in multiple countries. However, the more you expand outside your domestic homeplace, the greater the risks of misunderstanding different business environments, clashing cultures (both national and corporate), and escalating tensions between your team and those in other organizations. This is far from an easy path to travel. But it is also far from an impossible path to traverse.

After all, globalization is here to stay. While organizational hiccups will appear, international trade and partnerships will continue to grow.

Politicians, investors, and pundits have been ringing the death knell for globalization for decades. Many of these justifications have been based on the 2008 global financial crisis and the Covid-19 pandemic. However, the business world has successfully weathered both of these colossal events, albeit with a few scars, numerous business failures, and huge impacts on millions of people across the globe.

We also see greater diversification in global trade, not a decoupling driven by political issues and government tensions (even though, unfortunately, these will continue to increase). Of course, such growth will not be without hurdles, obstacles, and issues. We believe geopolitical tensions and intensified acrimonious government relations will continue to be a roller-coaster ride of escalation and de-escalation for decades.

However, stimulated by both the private and public sectors, global trade will continue to grow steadily for the foreseeable future. As a report from McKinsey in December 2022 noted, cross-border investments and global trade in goods and services continue to grow as we emerge from the pandemic. The world remains interconnected and interdependent.

So, where do you want to partner or do business? In your field of expertise, of course. While targeting the fast-growing technology and services sectors in the U.S. is tempting, also be sure to take notice of the manufacturing sector. While manufacturing only accounts for roughly 11% of the U.S. GDP, it consumes 20% of the country's capital investment, drives 60% of exports, and accounts for over 70% of business R&D spend.

The Changing American Business World

Before you start contacting prospective American partners or businesses, you need to understand how the American business world is changing and the implications of these changes.

Today's America is not the America of the 1990s or early 2000s. Many of these changes have slowly increased over the past 10-15 years. In most cases, acceleration escalated during and after the pandemic.

Additionally, the workplace is a blend of multiple generations that often clash and struggle to cooperate. They also bring differing values and viewpoints on communicating, using technology, and defining work ethics. For instance, the older generations value job security, personal recognition, and respect for authority. On the other hand, the younger generations prefer informal communication, using technology to communicate instead of conversations, and switching companies more frequently.

Millennials are the largest generation in the U.S. workforce today. Born between 1981 and 1996, they account for roughly one in three workers. However, by 2030, Millennials are estimated to comprise over 75% of the U.S. workforce.

Having almost entirely replaced their predecessor generations – Baby Boomers (1946-1964) and Generation X (1965-1980) – Millennials will be running the American corporate world within the next 7-10 years. Do you want a long-term partnership with American firms? Well, you had better start developing long-term relationships with the Millennials in these organizations, not just the senior-level executives they will soon replace.

At the same time, Generation Z (1997-2012) is entering the workforce. This generation is fully comfortable with technology and the digital world. The analog world is almost completely foreign to them. They have grown up with mobile phones and tablet devices in their hands almost since birth. Their ways of looking at the world and life are remarkably different, even from Millennials.

With this change of guard comes a change in values, beliefs, and perspectives on the general nature of business. Hopefully, it will also bring fewer cross-cultural biases and better approaches to conducting business. But that remains to be seen.

One significant change we are already witnessing with the Millennial Generation is that work may no longer be the number one priority in their lives. Working hard and long hours are values associated with the Baby Boomer Generation and, to a lesser extent, Gen X.

The realigned values of today's workforce have spurred the Great Resignation and Quiet Quitting trends. These trends make it more difficult to create lasting relationships with your counterparts in American firms, a troubling factor for those of you with cultural backgrounds that are more relationship-focused than task-focused.

This is more than just a U.S. phenomenon. In a recent research study by McKinsey in Europe of 16,000 people, one-third said they expected to quit their jobs within three to six months. The reasons cited included inadequate compensation, lack of career development and advancement, and uncaring and uninspiring leaders. Respondents said that the key motivators to stay on the job included flexibility, meaningful work, and supportive co-workers (factors that have grown in importance for Europeans during the pandemic).

One thing is for sure. You will need to develop multiple relationships at multiple levels to overcome these disquieting trends. Neither are short-term in nature, and both are highly likely to continue. While both these trends are impacting the world of business globally, they seem (at the moment) more pronounced and commonplace in the U.S.

A new, unnamed trend is adding more hurdles to building relationships with American workers: more Americans are choosing to work part-time. According to U.S. Labor Department data, over one million Americans joined the part-time workforce in December 2022 and January 2023. As of early 2023, over 22 million part-timers voluntarily worked less than 35 hours a week. This is over five times the four million who wanted full-time hours but could not get them. That is the highest ratio in two decades.

Why the change? The Labor Department says that more people are choosing to work part-time for "noneconomic reasons," such as caregiving and personal health. As noted above, work is no longer the number one priority for many people. Additionally, people no longer self-identify with their jobs or professions. Many have reframed their self-identity well beyond their roles in the workplace.

Another major change is how the younger generations want (and expect) to be treated in the workplace. While the examples below are admittedly a generalization, there is significant truth to these overall tendencies:

Baby Boomers – Respect My Title

Generation X – Respect My Ideas

Millennials – Respect My Skills

Generation Z – Respect Me for Whom I Am

Of course, each person you interact with is an individual, not a stereotype or generalization. However, there is no doubt that each generation has different values, wants, needs, and desires. You must accept and understand this, for you cannot change it.

The Future of Work

Two other trends that may change the American business environment in the near future are the four-day workweek and the continuation of hybrid working arrangements.

As of this writing, the direction of these trends is clear and concise. There has yet to be a major push for a four-day workweek in the U.S., but what about in your country?

Countries and businesses around the world have been trialing the four-day workweek in recent years. A 2019 study of UK businesses operating with a four-day workweek calculated an astonishing 92 billion pounds annual savings for the 250 participating companies.

Labor legislation worldwide is also changing rapidly. By the end of 2024, workers in Singapore will be entitled to request flexible work arrangements, including four-day work weeks, remote work, and flexible hours.

According to the World Economic Forum, a four-day workweek boosts employee productivity, as well as their mental and physical health. It also reduces CO_2 emissions, an important factor in global climate change. Speaking at the famed Davos meeting in January 2023, Sander van't Noordende, CEO of HR consulting firm Randstad, called the four-day working week "a business imperative."

If you move to a 4-day workweek and your counterparts in the U.S. do not, how might this impact your ability to partner and work with them? Americans like to have their overseas partners readily available to them (some would say too readily available!). Will your American colleagues be jealous of your long weekends? Will they become frustrated by the inability to contact you on 20% of their workdays? Will they understand and adapt to your working arrangements? That is not highly likely.

And what happens if, in a few years, U.S. businesses are pressured into a four-day workweek? That might be more plausible than it currently seems.

Not surprisingly, the four-day workweek is also highly popular with full-time workers. A survey by Bankrate of over 2300 U.S. adults found 81% "strongly or somewhat support" a four-day workweek, compared to 68% who support hybrid work and 64% who support fully remote work. The same survey revealed that over half (54%) of workers said they would be willing to work longer hours across four working days to have a four-day workweek. Interestingly, 37% said they would consider changing jobs, companies, or industries to attain a four-day workweek.

Again, this is not a U.S.-only trend. A four-day workweek trial in the U.K. from June to December 2022 involved 2900 employees from various industries. The average workweek was around 32 hours, and compensation remained the same.

The results showed that 71% of employees reported less burnout, 39% had less stress, and 60% enjoyed a better work-life balance. Additionally, fewer workers quit or took sick days compared to the same period in the previous year. It is little wonder that 92% of the companies participating in this six-month trial reported they would continue with the four-day workweek, with 30% saying it is a permanent change.

Is this a growing trend? Time will tell. However, legislators in Maryland have already proposed a five-year, four-day workweek pilot program in exchange for tax credits for participating businesses.

Bolt Financial tested the four-day workweek for three months and the results were reportedly overwhelmingly positive. So positive, in fact, that the company has embraced the change and adopted a four-day workweek for all employees as of January 1, 2022. Likewise, when social media management company Buffer tested the four-day workweek, 91% of employees stated they were happier and more productive.

Buffer has stated it is fully implementing the four-day workweek policy for the foreseeable future. Buffer CEO Joel Gascoigne stated, "*This 4-day workweek period is about well-being, mental health, and placing us as humans and our families first.*"

In another example, Exos, a performance coaching company with over 3500 staff, has implemented four-day work weeks since May 2023. Called "You Do You Fridays," employees choose how to spend each Friday. Some continue to spend part of the day working, but the vast majority take the day off. Executives at the company say this program has boosted productivity while reducing burnout, emotional exhaustion, and disconnect.

It will be interesting to see how much the momentum for a four-day workweek develops in the U.S. in the coming years. It will be an interesting experiment for many organizations!

Speaking of experiments, the hybrid and working-from-home (WFH) experience for many appears to be coming to an end, much to the displeasure of a significant portion of the American workforce. This is an interesting conundrum pitting senior executives and business owners against their middle and frontline managers.

Without a doubt, companies mandating full-time return-to-office policies are creating toxic relationships with their man of their employees. This portends a continuation of high employee turnover for these companies, especially when other organizations are willing to offer either full-time or part-time working-from-home arrangements. International executives and managers are likely to be extremely frustrated and irritated by continuously dealing with new people within their American partners.

Compounding this issue, employee engagement in the U.S. dropped to its lowest level in the first quarter of 2024 in over a decade, according to ongoing research from Gallup. Only 30% of U.S. workers were considered "highly engaged," and 17% were categorized as actively disengaged. These numbers likely foreshadow a continued negative impact on employee retention rates, productivity, and customer service.

However, as these two trends play out, there is no doubt that the future of work in the U.S. continues to evolve. Again, the impact of this evolution on your ability to build relationships with your American colleagues should not be underestimated. Importantly, these trends open immense opportunities for savvy international business executives and global companies to tap into.

CHAPTER 2

Business Culture Challenges

Across the globe, business cultures shape and influence accepted behavior as much as each national culture permits. Individuals at all levels of organizations constantly interact with one another without full knowledge and appreciation of these national, societal, and business cultural overlays influencing thoughts, behaviors, mindsets, biases, and actions.

Every business, though, is different and might not adhere to the same national culture, even though they have the same national origins. Since various factors, including individual leaders, regulations, workplace diversity, business requirements, and customer bases, affect corporate culture, international businesses must maintain a high level of resiliency and agility to preserve and maintain the success of their partnerships.

It is necessary to distinguish between national, regional, corporate, and individual cultures. Despite having many common ideals, American corporate cultures all follow different paths to autonomously and creatively develop their own distinctive cultures. Because of this, organizations like Microsoft and Google have moved away from formal, conservative corporate cultures and toward more relaxed, informal work environments. An extraterrestrial observing Earth might characterize human civilization as a single entity. Not until the extraterrestrial takes out a magnifying glass and focuses it on a specific area does it realize that there are numerous subcultures, including those based on gender, religion, status, and national, regional, and individual cultures.

For instance, in American society, where creativity and freedom of expression are valued highly, innovation is considered a key component of individual and corporate success. Thus, you will find more risk-takers and people willing to express ideas and propose solutions in American firms. It is not surprising to witness a junior employee sharing their ideas, opinions, and thoughts in a meeting. This can be unheard of in highly hierarchical societies and organizations where typically only senior managers talk and junior staff sit quietly and listen.

Significant changes have occurred in American companies in recent years regarding leadership and working conditions. Many of these changes were underway before the Covid-19 pandemic, but today, the changes are operating on steroids. Thirty years ago, the American workplace lacked diversity and was more homogeneous. Today, it is not uncommon to have diverse workers in leadership positions across the workforce. When there is diversity in the workplace, the corporate culture is organically impacted and adapts to reflect the distinctive qualities of each represented culture.

Numerous outside elements can impact business culture. Some are forced on corporations through laws and regulations (such as environmental protection legislation). Other changes result from societal pressures, particularly around issues such as diversity, equity, inclusion, accessibility, and working conditions. American businesses are expected to follow state and national laws.

External elements that impact a company's corporate culture include the business environment, supplier and consumer cultures, national legal systems, and the kinds of goods and services offered. Prosperous American corporations foster inclusive and friendly work environments that enable accomplished minorities to thrive and contribute to the company's operations. Because of this, international companies must research and comprehend the corporate cultures of their potential American partners, suppliers, and customers.

Agility and Adaptation

People from every country on the planet aspire to be valued for their cultures. The proverb "When in Rome, do as the Romans do" also applies to America. This is particularly significant given America's decades-long success. To succeed, follow the lead of the accomplished!

Does this advice apply to foreign businesses that intend to collaborate with U.S. businesses? If the response is in the affirmative, what kinds of actions foster enduring partnerships with American companies? What does an American define as "genuine?"

Regretfully, a sizable portion of American business executives express discontent when businesspeople from other cultures fail to adjust to and adopt the American business culture, which many Americans consider the standard for doing business globally. They contend that the American approach to business is the most effective global business culture. Why not? For many years, America has been the global leader, with other countries trying to follow suit by adopting English as their corporate language.

Since the American business model has proven effective, international corporations make every effort to collaborate with American companies. However, it is not as simple as it seems. When negotiating with Americans, should a Chinese business leader act like an American or a Chinese? What if the American corporate executive has previously studied and applied Chinese culture and negotiating strategies? Did they simply switch places while keeping the same space between them? Understanding and appreciating another's culture is much deeper than just trying to emulate that culture.

A Japanese customer once told one of the American authors of this book, "It is nice to see that you don't attempt to be more Japanese than I am! Thank you for becoming knowledgeable about our traditions and beliefs." When pressed for further details, the Japanese customer responded that while the Do's and Don'ts are crucial, having a sincere desire to engage on both an intellectual and emotional level with people from different cultures is just as vital.

Most prosperous immigrants to America choose to let go of the cultural programming they had growing up and become more accepting of the American culture. The desire to break free from the confines of their own cultures to provide a better future for their offspring is the source of their common values.

However, many places in the U.S. exist where individuals from different cultures congregate and exclusively speak their original language with their children. Initially, doing so provides a safe sanctuary to help them survive the cultural shock of moving to a new country. Unfortunately, when these children start interacting with the rest of society, they are at a significant disadvantage. The same is true for international corporations.

Effective global leaders know exactly how to collaborate with other businesses. Leaders have only two options: 1) Make their bank account balance larger by adapting to their partners' business cultures and ways of doing business, or 2) Change their partner's culture. They cannot do both! The second option is unlikely to succeed in the short or long term.

When conducting business, it is unnecessary to entirely give up one's cultural values to adapt to other cultures. Going global allows us to learn about the thoughts and emotions of leaders raised in diverse cultural contexts without adopting them. This implies that foreign businesses are more likely to thrive and form enduring relationships when they comprehend how Americans conduct business.

America's Unique Business Environment

There are many aspects of the American business environment and culture that you must become familiar with. Among these are:

- The American corporate culture often transcends national cultures, especially outside the United States.

- Empowered decision-making is fundamental to how U.S. companies operate.

- Americans take pride in their corporate brands.

- Egalitarianism is not as prevalent in all American organizations as you might think.

- Relationships tend to be built after the business deal is signed.

- The notion of "time is money" is more prevalent and important than you might realize.

We will delve into many cultural idiosyncrasies throughout the book. But now, here are some key points to keep in mind.

The power of American corporate culture is enormous. It often devours national cultures when U.S. businesses operate overseas. So, when dealing with the local subsidiary of an American firm, you might think that the national culture would prevail since most of the employees are local citizens who grew up in the national culture. However, that would be wrongful thinking.

For example, one of us was the Vice President of Marketing at Citibank in Singapore. Over 98% of the staff were local hires, with only a handful of expatriates. However, they more readily identified with the Citibank culture than many aspects of the local Singaporean culture.

Hence, Citibank's workplace culture in Singapore significantly differed from that of the local banks, where the local Singaporean culture predominated. For example, the local banks were much more hierarchical in their decision-making process, typical of most Asian cultures. At Citibank, decisions were readily pushed down to the manager and Assistant Vice President levels, with only the most strategic decisions being discussed at the Vice President leadership team level.

Anyone who dealt with Citibank in Singapore would have seen few differences in their experiences when engaging with the bank in Chicago, Hong Kong, or Mexico City. The corporate culture was that prevalent and powerful.

As in this example, empowered decision-making is entrenched within the American corporate culture. One thing to understand, however, is that in numerous organizations, this translates as empowered recommendation-making, not final decision-making. Yes, many decisions are delegated to the lowest level of the organization possible. But this is not always the case. Negotiated deals must often be "run up the flagpole" for higher-level approval. This can be very frustrating and damages relationships built through the negotiation process.

For example, co-author Steven was the Regional Director for TIME Magazine in South Asia. He had created and negotiated a special marketing promotion with his biggest client, Singapore Airlines (SIA), to celebrate the airline's 25th birthday. Unfortunately, when the promotion concept and budget were submitted to higher-level executives in TIME, they modified the deal beyond what was acceptable to SIA. As a result, archrival Newsweek secured the anniversary celebration promotion with SIA. His relationship (and the magazine's) with Singapore Airlines was never the same.

Corporate Culture Differences

Americans take significant pride in their companies, something which is unmatched elsewhere in the world

29

(with the possible exception of Japan). More corporate-branded merchandise (hats, jackets, coffee mugs, notepads, key chains, etc.) is manufactured for American corporations than anywhere else. Americans wear and use these logo-infused products with pride and delight.

What does this mean for you? Noting and commenting on the branding of your prospective partner or customer is vital. Always treat any corporate-branded merchandise given to you with the utmost respect. Likewise, making disparaging remarks about their branded merchandise is a definite no-no (believe us, we have seen people do this countless times). While these branded items may seem extravagant or even humorous to you, simply accept this as a fundamental part of the American business culture.

Another display of this corporate pride is how Americans identify themselves with their employers. Ask an American, "*What do you do?*" and the reply will often be along the lines of "*I work for IBM*" or "*I work for Boeing.*" Ask that same question of a European or Asian and the response is more likely to be, "*I am an engineer,*" or "*I am in finance.*"

As highlighted later in the book, the American social culture is highly egalitarian and informal. People are called by their given (first) names in most business and social settings. Also, remember the point above about the corporate culture subduing national cultures. This applies to the U.S. firms with offices and facilities outside the U.S. American firms in Germany, Switzerland, Mexico, India, China, Singapore, and Japan (for example) will be more egalitarian than their national counterparts.

Be forewarned, however, that even though the corporate culture in most U.S. firms is egalitarian, many U.S. organizations remain extremely hierarchical. Once people in these organizations reach the upper echelons, they are no longer called by their first names. Instead, you are more likely to hear "Mr. King" or "Miss Falcone." When these senior people are in a meeting room, lower-ranked employees will defer to them and withhold any contrarian thoughts and views. In some ways, these hierarchical organizations are the exceptions that prove the rule.

Another difference between Americans and the rest of the world is that Americans prefer to build relationships only after a business arrangement has begun. You are more likely to be invited for a round of golf after a contract is signed than during the negotiation phase.

On the opposite end of the spectrum, relationship building is integral to the negotiation process in many other parts of the world. This is why Americans like to visit your countries during negotiations. They get to play golf with you (at your invitation) before the deal is done!

Lastly, the phrase "time is money" has profound, deep-seated relevance for Americans. Americans do not like delays, people being late, inconveniences, or conversations that do not get to the business matter quickly. While this may make Americans appear blunt and cold, their eyes and minds are often squarely focused on time and duration. For them, the investment of their time needs to have a return (ROTI – return on time invested). Anything that takes longer than anticipated is an irritation.

Remember that showing your American partner how much you value them is demonstrated by your timely completion of tasks and delivering on your commitments.

31

Americans welcome and appreciate it when an international partner communicates early on that they believe they cannot meet stipulated deadlines. Americans view transparency as a leadership and confidence-boosting quality. Major damage to trust occurs when an international partner waits until the last minute to inform or act.

There are unique aspects to the business cultures in all countries worldwide. Our intention is not to cover these in this book. Instead, we want to ensure that you become aware of – and fully understand the implications of – the many unique aspects of the American business culture. Doing so will enhance your prospects for creating successful partnerships, joint ventures, and supplier relationships with American-based firms and their employees.

Here are some recommendations that may help open doors for your company:

- Connect with your country's embassy located in the United States.

- Reach out and build good relationships with the American embassy or consulate in your country to determine which American firms are interested in doing business with your country.

- Connect with your government and offer your services to US firms. Many countries have agreements with the United States to build business relationships between both countries.

- Attend trade shows, conferences, and symposiums to showcase your products and services expertise.

- Connect with companies in your country that have already established a working relationship with American firms. Offer to be a second-tier supplier to get closer to the American firms.

- Connect with competitors of American companies in your country and offer your services.

- Reach out to local universities and find out if they have internship programs with American firms. Then, offer to help or/and sponsor students working on projects of interest to American firms.

- Be active on professional social media (such as LinkedIn) by sharing your products and services to be noticed by American firms.

- Connect with leaders and employees on LinkedIn and other professional social media sites.

Project Management

The main components of traditional project management are requirement definition, planning, initiating, executing, controlling, and closure. The objective is to deliver high-quality goods or services on schedule and within budget.

The authors have seen many global executives avoid appearing inexperienced by not raising their concerns in the early stages of project management. Regretfully, a lack of understanding of the project scope and definition often results in the needless expenditure of time and resources to revise and clarify requirements mid-project. Usually, this damages relationships and trust with American executives and managers.

Both authors have observed and participated in numerous pointless follow-up meetings between international and American teams where the project description was piecemealed. It is unfortunate when the international partner and the American company wait until a project is almost completed before realizing that the foundation was laid incorrectly.

Micromanagement

Compared to workers from other cultures, Americans would rather work independently and without being micromanaged. Germany, Canada, and Australia are the only nations more independent than the U.S.

While their international counterparts welcome sporadic check-ins, American leaders or workers do not appreciate continuous interruptions or unscheduled check-in sessions. They will ask questions only if they have any. Workers and managers in Brazil and India, in particular, are accustomed to handling micromanagement better since they view the check-ins as an indication of caring.

Be alert for clues and expressions indicating an American wants you to get more involved in their activities and processes. As long as the finished product is well-defined, leave them alone. While you should be available to answer inquiries, avoid stifling them by glancing over their shoulders.

Contracts

Whether it is an official contract or an informal agreement, Americans value following through on agreements. Americans hold contracts in high regard, while people in other cultures often view these as starting points where the contracts can get modified as needed! They contend that since they and the other party drafted the agreement based on mutual respect and a positive working relationship, there is no reason not to alter it to uphold or enhance that mutual respect and trust.

While some Americans think it is okay to alter the plan, most Americans might think it disrespectful to amend contracts and often insist on contractually sticking to the original agreement.

Compared to many other countries, America's legal system is robust. No checks should bounce, no contract modifications should be made during a project's life cycle, and no payment delays should occur.

Here is a list of recommendations that will positively impact your partnership with American firms:

- Determine your American partners' strengths and weaknesses and how you can augment those strengths and aid them in closing gap areas. This becomes your value-add proposition.

- Collaborate with your American partner to establish communication standards and expectations.

- Find answers to the following questions:

- How soon after they send you an email should you reply?

- How should the burden of time zone differences be handled?

- How do you plan to deal with missed deadlines?

- How are you going to define what is truly urgent?

- How does your American counterpart make decisions?

- To whom and how should issues be raised and addressed?

- Possess Mental and Emotional Sturdiness

- Accept complexity.

- Identify worst-case scenarios and devise plans to prevent these or fix them if they arise.

- Be open-minded and believe in what American philosopher Richard Rorty calls "the perspective of perspectives," the ability to see another person's perspectives without changing one's perspective.

- Learn to adapt, be flexible, and be agile.

- Be sincere in your appreciation of American culture.

- Be willing to alter your behavior temporarily.

- Recognize that "No serious relationship" does not imply "No relationship."

- Consider the bigger picture and longer-term desirable outcomes.

- Listen beyond what is said, especially to what was not said.

- Remember that a lack of expressed gratitude does not imply that a relationship does not exist. Overtly expressing gratitude is not a fundamental element of American business culture.

The next chapter will cover additional business culture challenges you will likely face when dealing with American businesspeople.

CHAPTER 3

Challenges of Working with American Businesspeople

International executives and business leaders rightfully regard themselves as equal partners and anticipate the same in return from American leaders. On the other hand, American leaders expect international executives to be well-versed in American corporate culture. This forces international executives to decide between being rich and being right. For this reason, international executives must be open to learning new ways of doing business without breaking their company's policies.

Before creating partnerships with American companies, it is vital to discuss commonalities and differences in business practices, acceptable behavior, communication styles and frequency, and project management processes. To create and sustain a successful partnership, it is necessary to identify, understand, and accept any differences—and then agree on how to handle such differences.

Additionally, it is essential to understand which cultural aspects and customs their American partners fervently adhere to. Again, this will be unique to each corporate culture and individual preference. An astute international corporation must examine the American company's culture not as an organization but as individuals with distinct personalities. The secret is to learn how to build and maintain trust, mutual respect, and a solid working relationship with each of your counterparts within the American partner organization.

These are just a few of the fundamental elements that will enable you to navigate cultural differences, reach win-win outcomes, and ensure long-term partnerships with your American counterparts.

The two authors of *Partnering Successfully With American Firms* have observed international businesses interacting with American businesses in a wide variety of great and not-so-great ways.

Experience has shown that American firms expect international companies to bend over backward to accommodate their wants and needs. As discussed before, the large and growing supply of international companies wanting to do business with American firms provides American firms with a greater variety of options from which to choose. This results in much greater pressure on international companies to differentiate themselves from the rest of their global, regional, and U.S. domestic competitors.

To ensure successful partnerships, international leaders must become as knowledgeable as possible about American companies, emphasize their accomplishments, and turn their setbacks into valuable lessons before forming partnerships with them. Sharing your company's vision, objectives, and accomplishments with American business leaders and providing official documentation to support your successes is a sound way to establish credibility. American business leaders prefer collaborating with well-established foreign businesses led by highly self-aware and self-assured individuals.

Partnerships arise when people share a desire to grow their businesses by joining forces and supporting each other in achieving shared objectives. They function as both clients and suppliers. Whether a corporation is American or international, it aims to deliver high-quality products on schedule and within budget. In doing so, a worldwide business can transform commercial transactions into partnerships and mutually beneficial connections by being a good customer or supplier. At that point, the American partner will be more willing to cooperate or partner with the international business.

A better understanding of American corporate cultures brings international companies closer to success in starting a partnership with American firms. So, what are some misunderstood perceptions by international companies of American firms and American culture?

Areas likely to hinder the establishment of a healthy business relationship with American firms and that often go unnoticed or dismissed by international corporate leaders include :

- International leaders lacking an understanding of how and why adhering to project management practices, including project requirement definition, objective, initiating, planning, controlling, and closing, is critical to American firms.

- International leaders not recognizing that American leaders and workers often value time more than money.

- International leaders not understanding that speaking up to voice concerns, sharing bad news, and asking questions at the beginning of the project is acceptable and expected.

- Expectations of American firms of their international partners to make quick decisions, ask for help, and request clarifications on processes, requirements, and deliverables.

- International leaders feeling uncomfortable hearing their American partners constantly flaunting their success and business achievements.

- International leaders feeling awkward and uncomfortable working with less hierarchical organizations and with the tendency of Americans to use first names comfortably and dispense with titles or honorifics.

Successful global leaders are usually aware of the goals, values, and mission of American corporations. They send strong messages and deliver excellent products or services early in the partnership. Just like astute diners at restaurants take an unusual step, international leaders communicate indirectly to the American firm that they will benefit tremendously later in the partnership. As the father of co-author Ali pointed out, shrewd patrons will alert the restaurant waiter when they are good tippers. They communicate early to them, either by spoken or nonverbal cues, that they anticipate excellent treatment and will leave a generous tip for the server.

They would not wait until after dinner to ask to speak with the manager and let them know how happy they were. They would perform that early on in the evening. Ali's father advised him that if he left a tip for someone as soon as he entered a restaurant, word would go out to the chef and the kitchen staff. When you do that, the server will work extremely hard to exceed your expectations. It has been said before, "No one rises to low expectations," which is very true concerning partnerships between international and American firms.

Unintentional Faux Pas

International business leaders often find Americans to be culturally rude, insensitive, obtuse, and tactless.

Be advised: this is not due to upbringing, feelings of superiority, or jingoism. Rather, it is a matter of naïveté. It stems from a general lack of international experience and knowledge. Unfortunately, it often results in unintentional cultural faux pas being committed.

Here is a story from co-author Steven and his experience when accompanying an American client to Japan:

> My client and I were researching hotels in Japan for a major regional conference for the client's company. I was their consultant and responsible for organizing this annual meeting for over 1200 of their clients and partners in the Asia/Pacific region.
>
> My client was new to Asia (and fairly new to me), and it was her first trip to Japan. I had been living in Singapore for over six years at that time and had made many previous business trips to Japan.

There is a formality to exchanging business cards in Japan, of which my client was unaware.

During the first three meetings, my client kept putting the business cards handed to her immediately in her notebook. I, on the other hand, followed protocol, looked at each card diligently, and commented on each. Then, as is customary, I placed them on the table in front of me.

I hoped she would pick up on my actions, but she did not. As Japan has a highly male-centric business culture, the Japanese managers focused their presentations and comments on me. I had to keep motioning to them to direct these to her, especially since she was the client and I was in an advisory role.

Unfortunately, she also kept referring to the Japanese managers by their first names instead of the more formal use of family names followed by "san," as in "Miki-san."

Their actions frustrated her since she was the ultimate decision-maker and represented the firm hosting the event. She felt overlooked and ignored, and rightfully so. But, at the same time, she was disrespecting Japanese culture and these business leaders in their own country (and in front of their subordinates attending the meetings).

She vented her frustrations to me at lunchtime. Fortunately, I could explain to her the cultural differences (national and business cultures) that were happening. I taught her the protocol for exchanging business cards, the importance of referring to Japanese managers by the "family name plus san" practice, and even how to bow politely at the end of each meeting (and the order for doing so).

She did not intend to offend anyone. She was simply unaware of these Japanese customs and business practices. Fortunately, she quickly understood how to be culturally flexible and agile, and eventually, she became quite comfortable engaging with Japanese customers and vendors.

The important thing to remember is that most Americans will appreciate being told – quietly and in private – when they are making cultural faux pas. They never intend to offend anyone or be rude intentionally. In fact, it is just the opposite. Being so open and easy-going, they simply anticipate that everyone else is just the same...at least until they start having international business experiences!

Relationships vs. Business

Many International leaders believe that American leaders put business issues, tasks, and accomplishments before establishing relationships, which is usually completely correct. However, it is important to understand that American companies enhance and strengthen business relationships over time based on work ethics, open communications, and keeping commitments.

Other cultures may start by focusing on the relationship based on recommendations from trusted sources and then expect work deliverables and schedules to be modified to keep the relationship intact. Their emphasis prioritizes building and maintaining the relationship, with business matters receiving secondary priority.

Most American firms place high importance on business practices because, for them, that is the true test of a healthy partnership. Confidence increases between American leaders and their international counterparts when international corporations fulfill their agreements, promises, and commitments.

Here is an example from co-author Steven's experiences in Asia. As mentioned above, he spent several years as the meeting organizer for his client's annual Asia/Pacific conference of clients and partners, which rotated around the region each year.

The first event was held in Manila, and he hired a multimedia company in the Philippines to create the staging, lighting, screens, and backdrop. "My engagement with this company was strictly professional that first year," recalls Steven. "Although they frequently invited me to stay for a weekend and visit other parts of the country with them, I always declined. I did not want to be seen as someone whose business judgment and decisions might be influenced by these trips."

He goes on with the rest of the story:

> We did hold a celebratory dinner with their whole team and my client at the end of this four-day event in Manila. Both the client and I were extremely pleased with the quality of their execution before and during the event. To say the least, it was a highly successful event, and they were a key reason for it.

The following year, the event was held in Bangkok. I got the Filipino company to provide a quote and solicited another from a company in Thailand. We elected to go with the Filipino company again, even though they meant covering their travel costs. Again, their performance was excellent.

In the following years, this annual conference was held in Malaysia, Korea, Japan, and Hong Kong. We never again asked for a competitive quote from other suppliers. Of course, we always negotiated on price and deliverables.

The relationship with the company in Manila got stronger with each subsequent year. As long as they kept performing to expectations, both the client and I were happy to continue engaging them. The nice thing is...they never let us down!

Over the years, they also received other multi-media projects from the client and I was happy to recommend them to my other clients. We also become friends, eventually holidaying together and getting to know each other's families and histories.

This is a good example of how a successful business partnership between an American firm (Steven's client), an experienced American expatriate businessperson, and an international company can turn into long-term business and personal relationships. Like Steven and his client, however, it first starts with a prescribed and conventional business exchange.

Interestingly, this is not the fundamental way of conducting business in much of the world (which often shocks American leaders and managers first entering the international business space). For example, in nations like China, Kuwait, Saudi Arabia, Mexico, and Ethiopia, the business mindset is centered on the belief that excellent business outcomes flow from relationships. The focus on developing relationships through business – rather than developing business through relationships – is more predominant in the U.S., Russia, the U.K., and Sweden.

Hence, leaders from Saudi Arabia, Japan, China, the Netherlands, Mexico, and other countries should not get upset if an American visiting team leaves immediately after a meeting ends to board an early flight home. Americans do not intend to offend their international partners. Rather, they act this way because they focus only on honoring their business commitments when meeting others.

For Americans, a business trip is just that: a trip to execute business meetings and make business decisions. Taking time for relationship-building after the meetings conclude is not part of the equation.

Remember, for Americans, "time is money." They are typically in a hurry to rush off to the next business opportunity. Also, they may not want to be seen back home as enjoying "vacation time" on company time or money. Hence, they are reluctant to stay a few extra days to learn and appreciate your culture, history, cuisine, or customs. One of the biggest wishes of many American leaders is for others to understand and appreciate this American business mindset.

Collaboration Challenges

When international companies enter into joint ventures with American firms, one of the mistakes they often make is basing their decision on how the CEOs or senior executives of the two companies collaborate and get along. When senior leaders from different companies discuss collaborating, they might not see potential execution difficulties because they have so much in common. After all, these executives usually get their positions due to their global mindsets and abilities to transact business across borders.

Many international business leaders have attended American universities and lived in the United States. Or they have years of experience working with American colleagues in their own or other firms. American leaders recognize and respect these "Americanized" traits in their counterparts, thinking, "This is a person we can do business with." This can lead these leaders, in both American and international companies, to downplay or dismiss cultural differences.

However, when the middle manager employees from both companies start to collaborate, cultural issues begin to percolate and escalate. That is where the rubber meets the road, and unfortunately, the strategies and plans do not work out as desired. Cross-cultural communication issues are often the root cause of collaboration and execution problems.

Communication

There are two types of communication: direct and indirect.

The use of direct and indirect communication differs widely across the globe. For instance, people in China, India, or Japan would rather be indirect and appear discreet and respectful. This also applies to people from these nations working in companies outside their native countries, especially if they have been expatriates for less than five years. Their home-grown, national cultural tendencies remain strong within them.

Because it is hard for Americans to read the non-verbal signals of non-Americans, this frequently produces problems. As direct communicators, Americans tend to interact with others straightforwardly. Unfortunately, they often expect the same in return, which rarely happens with people from collectivistic, hierarchical, or indict communicating societies.

Americans tend to smile easily and greet guests with enthusiasm. This exuberance of expressing gratitude and optimism can be off-putting to those from more reserved cultures. For example, the Dutch could view this as dishonest and phony, while the Russians might see it as an indication of ineptitude. Again, the importance of understanding one another and each person's cultural background cannot be overstated.

Americans do not like to mince words and prefer to communicate directly and to the point! Instead of sailing in a lake of silence, they prefer to do so in an ocean of words. Because of this, people from cultures such as the Japanese, who communicate with a high context and implicit method, are surprised when an American communicates directly with a low context and explicit approach. Navigating these different styles of communication is an art!

Americans aim to build on whatever they see as a good foundation to produce excellent business outcomes. They want to know upfront about any hurdles and obstacles to success. People who sidestep difficult issues and subjects and let others interpret what is being said are typically disliked (and distrusted) by Americans.

Profit is good for business. Time is money. So, they want to know what might impact profitability and anything that might cause delays, reworks, course corrections, and other time wasters. The best practice is to get quickly to the point! Transparency is appreciated by American businesspeople and is viewed as a foundation of mutual trust. If something is of concern or bothers you, raise it directly. Refrain from leaving unattended misinterpretations or different understanding of words or phrases. Clarify, clarify, clarify at all times.

To demonstrate the immense impact of word selection, here is a real-world situation encountered by co-author Ali. During a meeting between an American company and an Italian firm, the American presenter used the word "eventually" to describe the arrival of parts from the American company to the international firm in Rome.

Every time the American presenter used that word, the Italian frowned and looked concerned. After the end of the meeting, the Italian representative approached Ali and voiced his displeasure at the likelihood that the Italian firm would not receive the needed parts. When investigating the possible cause of the miscommunication, Ali realized that for Americans, "eventually" means that the parts will undoubtedly arrive in Rome at some point.

However, the Italian representative had a different meaning of the word. For Italians, the word "eventually" conjures up the word "eventualità," which means "there is a possibility this might or might not happen." The Italian representative erroneously understood that the parts may or may not arrive.

Effective Communication

Effective communication requires more effort than Efficient communication!

Let's go back in time and examine how we develop our communication skills from the time we were infants until we reach adulthood. Newly born babies interact with the world they get dropped into in several ways: they get scared when they hear loud sounds, when they get hungry, when they need to relieve themselves, and when they feel they are about to fall. None of our fears or perceptions as adults were with us at that earlier age.

We start projecting meaning to objects and people's behavior as we exercise our five senses. Imagine an infant surrounded by their parents who provide them with all kinds of verbal and nonverbal clues. The most precious time of these proud parents comes when the infant says "ma" or "da." As we know, infants at that early time make all sorts of sounds and voices that go unnoticed until they say a word that rhymes with "ma" or "da." That is when the parents react, and the infant receives verbal and nonverbal affirmation and appreciation for what they did. The infant undoubtedly thinks, "Hey, I don't know what I just said, but I am going to keep saying it."

That is when infants start filling their toolbox with words or sounds and attach meanings to those words and sounds. They keep filling their toolbox with words based on the culture of parents, siblings, friends, teachers, and others. Americans and international companies are no different. International and American firms have filled their respective communications and corporate culture boxes with many idioms, acronyms, processes, best practices, and acceptable behaviors.

Defining what is in each box before embarking on any partnership will undoubtedly reduce the possibility of misunderstandings. For example, will you use the metric or the English systems of measurement? When using numbers, is the decimal depicted as a period (.) or a coma (,)?

So far, so good. But what is the preferred method of communication for American firms? The answer is simply "it depends." It depends on the phase of the project and the formality of the transaction or arrangement. Unwritten contracts are nothing but small talk and informal. They are just conversations, period!

Efficient communication occurs when one person encodes an idea into a series of lined-up words from their toolbox of words to send them to another person. The other person receives that series of words and compares them to the words from their toolbox to encode them and reconstruct the idea accordingly. The closer the meaning of the words in both boxes, the better!

When words or phrases have different meanings or interpretations across cultures, communications can go astray, as in the story above about "eventually."

Even having similar communication toolboxes does not guarantee effective communication. You may have witnessed people talking with each other while speaking the same language, yet they truly do not communicate with one another. They know exactly how to encode and decode an insult, but is that effective in making the relationship and partnerships conducive to success? Absolutely not!

You may have met couples who have been in love for years, but communication in their early years together was mainly non-verbal since they spoke different languages, yet they were happy. A friend of co-author Ali recently married a Brazilian lady. Neither of them spoke the other's native language when they first met.

They probably would not have made it to the altar if Google Translate had not assisted during their dates. They employed their non-verbal skills, which proved a great asset, even after the wife became fluent in English. Since their hearts listened to each other more than their ears, they bonded beautifully. What does this have to do with partnering with American firms? Everything!

When leaders from American firms know and witness your genuine interest through your words and actions, hiccups become opportunities to build and strengthen trust. When what is important to your American partner is important to you, there will be a wide range of possibilities for a successful partnership.

However, calm seas do not make great sailors. Hence, problem-free partnerships do not always move the relationship from the initial zone of satisfaction into the zone of loyalty. In summary, it is not what is said or done that matters the most. How it is said and done lifts relationships to higher levels or sends them plummeting to unwelcomed depths.

To provide more examples of effective communication, the following are several areas that we encourage international companies to pay attention to.

Email

Americans seek efficiency, productivity, and quick results, which stems from the cultural dimension that time is precious. Therefore, one can imagine how frustrating it is for an American, especially from the younger generations, to receive a very long email or video clip. That perspective resulted in the acronym TLDR, which stands for Too Long, Didn't Read!

Here is a perfect example of how emails are viewed differently between international and American firms. Co-author Ali used to support international and American airline customers. A valuable lesson he learned occurred when he contrasted and analyzed the emails received from Asian customers and compared these with emails from American customers.

If airline staff from America and Asia ask the same question, efficiency calls for drafting the same response and sending it to both. However, the lesson learned is that responses will be regarded differently by culturally different recipients.

Asian customers are usually not as direct in their communication as Americans. For this reason, it is more effective to write a more detailed email to the Asian customer explaining the findings and determining factors that led to a negative reply to their request. When writing to individuals from high-context cultures, it is recommended that the last paragraph of the email conclude with something like "For the above reasons, we cannot grant permission to ...".

Asian and other high-context cultures appreciate softening the blow in the response. These cultures characteristically value harmony and indirect communication. A detailed response explaining the rationale for a decision will be perfect for the face-saving cultures in Asia.

However, that approach might get an American screaming, "Get to the point! Stop circling the airport and land the airplane!" An American would explain further, "Just tell me the answer: yes or no. If I want more details, I will ask."

Another interesting fact about Americans writing emails is that they do not feel it is necessary to open with or include small talk. They feel there is little or no need to start with a "good morning" or "I hope you had a good weekend" phrase.

Rather, their focus is, you guessed it, efficiency. The American thought process of writing emails goes along the lines of: why would I communicate my appreciation every time I write an email when we have already established a good working relationship? A simple "Hi" should be sufficient. They know I care about them.

Their intent is not to be rude or offensive. Their focus on extreme efficiency is the justification.

To give you another great example of where efficiency can harm effectiveness and relationships, one of co-author Ali's Italian-American friends, who worked with him in the same company, once shared:

> While working one Monday morning, I got a phone call from an Italian customer who asked me to rush to his office for an important matter. As soon as I walked into his office, I noticed he was uncomfortable and staring at an email on his laptop screen. He asked me to read an email that had arrived a few minutes earlier from an American engineer. He asked me why the American who sent him the email was upset.

I read the email and did not find it to be as perceived. All that the American engineer wrote was a direct reply to the question from the Italian customer. My Italian colleague then turned to me and asked, "How come he gave me the answer like this? No good morning. Nothing!"

At this point, I took the opportunity to explain the cultural differences and that the American correspondent was not upset and had no intention of being rude. Just efficient!

Of course, this does not apply to every American. However, it is common for emails to get straight to the point without friendly greetings or asking about the recipient's well-being. Even co-author Ali admits that American culture has influenced him to the point that others questioned if he was upset with them for being direct. It is an easy trap to fall into, particularly in today's hectic and rushed business environments.

Best Practices for Effective Communications

Here are tips for making your email communications with American businesspeople more effective:

- Be brief in your emails and share more information in attachments. This way, the reader will have the option of not reading the whole message.

- State the purpose of the email from the beginning. Is it a request for action or information only?

- Be specific and limit the email to one topic. Use a subject line that specifies the topic so the reader can readily locate it later if necessary.

- When emailing a group of people, specify who on the distribution should respond or decide. When everyone is in charge, no one is in charge!

- Answer a question at the beginning and follow it with justification if needed. And let the recipient know you will be happy to answer any questions.

In-Person Meetings

When it comes to in-person and face-to-face meetings with American businesspeople, best practices include:

- Invite those who care, know, can contribute to the discussion, can be sponsors, or have a stake in achieving the deliverables emanating from the meeting.

- Include in the email the following: the purpose of the meeting, background, supporting material, homework that needs to be completed before the meeting, specific deliverables, and the decision-making process to be used (command, vote, or consensus).

- Start the meeting with introductions, including names, titles, and company names (if not an internal discussion).

- Take meeting minutes, action items, and parking lot items for post-meeting distribution.

- At the end of the meeting, go over the action items and parking lot items by assigning action items to specific people, including the completion dates and specifying exact deliverables. This is known in American business culture as the 3Ws: Who will do What by When.

- State the purpose and timing of possible follow-up meetings.

- After the meeting, send the summary with all the above, including communicating dates and details of any follow-up meetings and expectations for communicating progress on action items.

Virtual Meetings and Conversations

Best practices for virtual meetings and conversations include:

- In addition to what was mentioned above for in-person meetings, mention your full name and company name when you speak for the first time. After that, mention only your first name and company unless other attendees have the same name. Set the expectation from your American audience to do the same.

- Speak slowly and clearly.

- Share background material before the meeting. The payback from doing this is much higher than for in-person meetings.

- Before the meeting begins, ensure the connection is strong and people can hear you clearly.

- Arrive 5-7 minutes early to test your camera and audio settings. This will also give you a little time to get to know the other participants before the meeting starts.

- Use an AI (artificial intelligence) tool for captioning, especially if the meeting is recorded.

- Be fully present. Put mobile phones on airplane mode. Turn off notifications on your computers and other devices. Close email and browsing apps that might distract you.

Idioms and Slang

While slang may seem natural and comfortable to the speaker, it may not make sense to the listener. During a recent trip, an American executive of a Fortune 500 business hurried to co-author Ali's office one afternoon to discuss the insights he had gained from his German clients. He claimed that the first request from the clients was for him to remind his American associates to refrain from using colloquialisms and sports lingo.

For non-Americans, statements like "This one is a slam dunk" may have no meaning. As we were writing this book, we tried to ensure that no American idioms made it to the final draft.

On the other hand, it is valuable to understand the importance of idioms since they effectively express ideas or concepts. One of the best ways for international leaders to display an in-depth knowledge of American culture is to use common idioms when appropriate. Of course, caution is necessary to know which idioms to use and to ensure no one is offended. Also, be warned that some idioms will not be well received, depending on where people work and live in the United States.

Note: The back of the book includes a list of common American idioms and business acronyms to help you fill your personal and corporate communications toolbox.

Hot Topics

Politics and religion are two topics that should be avoided at any cost. Co-author Ali witnessed an occurrence that showcases the importance of this recommendation.

During a dinner with an international customer, one of the engineers from the international team took the liberty to agree with one of the members of the American team concerning their views of a political figure in the United States. While the international team member felt great that he and the American team member agreed, Ali noticed the international team leader getting uncomfortable with their conversation.

After the dinner, Ali saw the international leader having a one-on-one discussion with his colleague, cautioning him that the Monday morning meeting might be difficult because some other members of the American team might have different political views than the international team member and the American.

The American political figure being discussed had polarized parts of the country, and it was likely that some members of the American team would also have conflicting views. This is why discussions around politics are best avoided, particularly in large group settings.

Negotiating with Your American Partner

When negotiating with your American partner, remember that several factors will impact your partnership, including communication styles, attitudes toward concessions, contract flexibility or rigidity, harmony, transparency, government influence, culture, legal systems, and adherence to the law. Except for national security and antitrust matters, the most common distinction between negotiations in the United States and the rest of the world may be summed up as the U.S. government's lack of intervention and rigid control. Negotiations in the United States are relatively quicker than in most other countries.

The intent of most American leaders the authors have worked with is to believe that most American negotiators work towards reaching a win-win outcome, unlike many other cultures. However, during negotiations, Americans tend to prioritize deadlines, which can work for you or against you as a potential partner. Also, your American counterparts will want to include specifics and tightly worded details in Statements of Work (SOWs), Letters of Agreement (LOAs), proposals, and contracts.

Just because you have a positive working relationship with American leaders does not mean they will make exceptions to the rules and specifications of contracts and agreements. Integrity and abiding by the rules are legally enforceable and thus fully embraced.

Since companies in the United States are becoming increasingly diverse, be extremely observant in learning the corporate culture and the cultural tendencies of the American individuals you are negotiating with.

How can an international company enhance its relationships with American businesses and businesspeople?

Prosperous multinational corporations ought to sincerely convey and demonstrate their gratitude for the connections with American enterprises from the outset of their business partnership. They can accomplish that by seizing every chance to emphasize the American company's excellent services, products, people, and leaders.

When you observe employees of an American company doing things appropriately or beyond expectations, please take notice of it and share this with your American counterparts at every opportunity. This will establish a reciprocal attitude of gratitude and cement your intention to offer the American company a first-rate service or product.

Gaining an understanding of American companies' core values – time, quality, exceeding expectations, and outstanding performance – will win them over as devoted partners. Additionally, by doing this, when it comes time to raise issues or concerns, your constructive criticism of the American corporation or a specific individual will have greater weight and legitimacy.

Co-author Ali once observed two international partners working with an American company in two very distinct ways. International firm A's representative was constantly grumbling about numerous things. He seized every chance to point out issues and argue that the American company's disregard for quality was the cause. Sadly, this continued for several months. Although it would have been damaging for the American corporation to end the partnership, it did not result in its termination.

However, employees from the American corporation dreaded interacting with this international representative. It came to a point where simply saying hello to him was avoided because of his unfriendly and constantly complaining attitude. Soon, the American employees would only complete the specific tasks assigned to them, even if there were instances when they could have done better or more.

Ali even observed that some of the American employees took vacations to avoid having to go to the international company's office and sit next to the representative. Needless to say, this was a joint-venture project with high levels of unanticipated risk due to this incompatible clash of national and personal cultures.

On the other hand, the representative for company B was quite kind and grateful. He was eager to see the American corporate employees doing things correctly. He often pointed out their outstanding work in emails to the employees, their bosses, and their senior management. Furthermore, he did not go above their heads to make anyone look awful when things went wrong. He always tried to solve problems at the lowest level of both organizations as possible.

Employees from the American firm were so appreciative that they would work extra hours and occasionally even on their vacations to help this international representative and company B. This was a great example of someone thoroughly understanding American society and knowing what Americans look for in a partnership.

Intangibles

Initial perceptions that you will be a reliable partner, supplier, or customer often impact the dynamics of partnerships. The adage "you will never get a second opportunity to make a good first impression" is one that we have all heard. This is particularly applicable to joint ventures between international and American businesses.

Confidence is one of the key ingredients to produce a fantastic first impression. Overconfidence, though, may not be a good idea. This fact applies to all cultures, not just the American culture. Although a foreign partner may show confidence, it will eventually be subject to the "trust but verify" policy many American leaders adhere to.

The abbreviation for responsibility, accountability, and authority (RAA) is well-known within American businesses. Accountability arises from the fact that effective communication is greatly valued. American businesses place a high priority on accountability.

What actions can international businesses take to create a positive first impression?

Specific actions include:

- Learn as much as possible about the American company, emphasizing its accomplishments and downplaying its shortcomings.

- Arrive on time and be prepared.

- Bring brochures or any other materials that highlight your company's goals, objectives, and track record of success.

- Inform the American company about your investments in the country and your stake in the partnership's success. The more loyal you seem to American companies, the better.

Summary

The most important advice for international leaders is to make Americans feel appreciated and valued. Although this is universal, Americans will only give you what you want as a partner when they know your mind and heart are with them. Having a mindset of gratitude takes you a long distance in the right direction.

Albert Einstein once said, "The most important question anyone could ask is, 'Is this a friendly universe?'" The same question applies to all business relationships, especially with customers and American firms.

The more you understand your programming from your culture, the smaller the cultural gap will be. An American partner being on time indicates they value the relationship. They will return the favor in ways you appreciate as long as you communicate what those criteria are. Adapting the American way of doing business does not mean you have to give up yours completely. But it may take some flexibility and adjustments. Win-win is the best way to view the partnership.

In the next chapter, we will share some cross-cultural dimensions and gaps you may encounter when partnering or doing business with American businesspeople.

CHAPTER 4

Cross-Cultural Gaps and Bridges

C ulture is the lens through which people view the world. It is central to how we each interpret situations, events, and communications. It is how we make sense of the workplace and the world around us.

In essence, a culture is a shared system of meanings, beliefs, values, and behaviors through which experiences are interpreted and interpersonal communication is formed.

The bottom line is simple: we do not see things as they are; we see them as we are!

The usual metaphor is to describe cultures as being like icebergs. What we see and notice at the surface of other people's cultures are things like dress, music, literature, arts, culinary, and sports. However, we do not see the critical elements below the surface, such as concepts related to status, fairness, justice, relationships, and hierarchy. Yet, when we consider the important elements of our own cultures, these are the essential factors we believe define us. Not surprisingly, these are also the elements that others use to define themselves, yet they often remain mysterious, unfamiliar, and unknown to us.

Added to the mixture of puzzling differences are the varied ways and importance that body language and context impact communication across the world.

Hence, cross-cultural awareness is the foundation of professional and personal communication and relationships. And this starts with becoming aware of our personal cultural values, beliefs, business practices, and perceptions.

The factors impacting the cultural make-up of individuals in the workplace are complex and two-fold: national and corporate.

The national factors include regional particularities, ethnicity, education, religion, gender, and life experiences. The corporate culture elements include workplace climate, how conflict is handled, collaboration practices, leadership styles, and peer pressure. The national culture factors result from collective programming from families, schools, societies, and laws. On the other hand, corporate culture foundations are learned and will change as people leave organizations for new ones.

Typical blocks to cultural communication and understanding include:

Ethnocentrism – the inability to accept another culture's worldview.

Discrimination – differential treatment of an individual due to status (actual and perceived).

Stereotyping – generalizing about a person while ignoring the presence of individual characteristics and differences.

Cultural blindness – differences are ignored and one proceeds as though the differences do not exist.

Cultural Imposition – the belief that everyone should conform to your culture's beliefs and values.

Tone Difference – being formal in tone and how others are addressed. While traditional and acceptable in some cultures, this can be perceived as embarrassing and off-putting to people from other cultures, resulting in "subservient" typecasting.

American Culture Overview

Despite being sometimes described as a "melting pot," American society is actually a salad made up of numerous subcultural ingredients! The subcultures are different, but they share a lot in common.

For instance, there is a strong cultural perspective on trust across almost all of American society, which strongly influences the extremely important role of trust in American business culture. Simply stated, Americans usually trust people who DO what they SAY and SAY what they DO.

People demonstrate competency, dependability, reliability, and integrity when they follow through on their promises. They exhibit transparency when they say what they think. Americans prioritize results and reciprocal business or financial advantages over relationships while displaying high rational objectivity. Results and outcomes foster confidence and build trust.

Credibility must be earned, not given! Data and facts liberate people and are considered the most effective tools for making decisions and reaching conclusions. Gaining trust begins with demonstrating intent through competence and expertise. In most cases, credentials – rather than connections – are why American firms recruit and hire people...and how they choose to partner with individuals and other business entities.

On the other hand, connections may be considered if they can offer information or examples demonstrating your legitimacy, competence, and reliability. The American proverb, "I love my mother, but I will not trust her to fly an airplane!" shows that Americans tend to abide by the "trust but verify" maxim.

For instance, Middle Easterners may place all their trust (*Thiqa*) in a person because of their ties to other reputable, far-off families or tribes. That characteristic is almost totally absent throughout American culture. However, recommendations by trusted sources might provide a push toward choosing a candidate for a job interview or consideration for a partnership.

Most Americans trust those who fulfill their promises by completing things on time or schedule. Raising the alert flag before an agreed schedule is at risk is a perfect example of the open, honest, and transparent communication Americans appreciate. For Americans, this is a deep-seated sign of respect for them personally and the partnership. Doing so shows that their counterparts understand that Americans deeply dislike surprises and hearing about problems that have escalated into major issues that could have been headed off earlier.

Maintaining constant communication about project progress reflects excellent leadership and promotes reliance and interest in working together more. Going the extra mile to exceed American expectations, regardless of whether you finish the project ahead of schedule, builds loyalty.

Exceeding expectations is always best, but even the intention of occasionally exceeding expectations is enough to bolster a strong relationship regardless of the ups and downs of business. Having said that, smart and experienced international leaders know that American companies are motivated more by profit now than later. Americans will not hesitate to drop a partner for a better one.

Therefore, the best advice is not to let your shield down and become complacent just because you have a partnership agreement in place. American companies will not feel remorse by ending a business relationship with a partner. Likewise, they expect the same to be done to them by their customers and partners if they do not keep their commitments.

Diving Deeper

The most important advice that international leaders could benefit from is to go beneath the surface and what is readily visible to understand what truly motivates Americans to do what they do. Similar to icebergs, cultures have more secrets beneath the surface than above. International leaders must set aside their cultural paradigms to learn the American way of doing business.

Ralph Lipton once said, "The person living at the bottom of the sea is the last person on Earth to understand water." Until international leaders dare to step outside their own cultures, even temporarily, they will not realize the gravity and nuances of their own cultural programming.

Differentiating between stereotypes, educated guesses, and generalizations is crucial. When done scientifically and with the support of solid facts, generalization is the lifeblood of science. It enables humans to minimize and perhaps completely eradicate the effects of the unknown. But if used carelessly and taken for granted without any wiggle room, it will result in stereotyping, where individuals reshape reality to suit their prejudicial (and often unfounded) viewpoints.

Business leaders will have a higher chance of succeeding when they recognize that the perceived directness of Germans, the tendency to interrupt during discussions by the French, the love of vagueness by Japanese, and the expressiveness of Italians are all non-combative. According to a generalization made by the former U.S. Federal Communications Commission chairman, Mr. Newton Minow, "Under the law, Germans believe that everything is forbidden until it is authorized, while French people believe that everything is allowed unless it is prohibited."

He added, "Everything is forbidden, even what the Russians are allowed to do, but the Italians believe everything is allowed, even the forbidden."

While there is some truth to this, it also presents both the issue and its remedy. Similarly, international companies will have greater opportunities to establish and sustain business links with American leaders if they understand and accept the widespread belief that

Americans prioritize business matters over professional and corporate relationships.

Icebergs

People resemble icebergs. The only features that are easily observed and evident are the obvious and exterior ones. You have to go deep to see beyond the surface. The outward features that catch our attention when we first meet someone are things like color, communication style, symbols, and those things that people feel are vital to disclose.

If we allow it, the environment we are raised in shapes who we are. Each member of society chooses to join the group and follow the rules established by the community.

In addition to events and how we respond to them, our identities are shaped by the influence of our parents, environments, friends, relatives, religions, societies, and our personal histories.

Our upbringing profoundly impacts our speech and behavior patterns, and we must spend the remainder of our lives unlearning and relinquishing the cultural programming we were exposed to. Our vocabulary grows from the words we hear and those we elect to keep in our communication toolbox.

Every day, from the minute we wake up until we sleep, we switch between three tasks: thinking, feeling, and doing. Our activities, albeit not always in this order, reveal who we are due to the things and mindsets we have gathered over time.

Our thoughts, feelings, and actions shape who we are. But how we reconsider these aspects shapes who we become! Our beliefs about who we are, what we believe others think of us, and the environment we take for granted all impact our thinking, doing, and feeling. Culture, attitude, environment, and many other elements influence our conduct. Becoming self-aware is the only way to change course and go in a new direction.

Computers and humans have so much in common, except that humans cannot control their eye color, hair type, or height. However, both computers and humans can be programmed. Computer programming is done with a software download, while humans are programmed by the cultural micro and macro-inequities absorbed and adopted into their mindsets and behaviors. Computers can be upgraded by uninstalling old software and installing new ones. Humans can also get upgraded, although not as easily, if they let go of old beliefs and unwanted programming they have been subjected to at an early age with new beliefs.

Happiness is the most common thing we pursue in life, from the moment we are born until we pass away. Money may be said to be our ultimate goal, but what benefits would money offer? Strength, freedom, and peace of mind are qualities directly connected to happiness. Our loved ones and surroundings also profoundly influence us as we age.

Global Cultural Dimensions

Aperian Global is a learning platform with over 30 years of extensive research and insights into understanding culturally diverse individuals, teams, and organizations. According to their research, Western cultures are usually far across the spectrum from other cultures across many cultural dimensions.

Western cultures, particularly the United States, UK, and Australia tend to be independent, egalitarian, risk-takers, direct communicators, and task-oriented. Many other cultures lean towards being interdependent, status-oriented, risk-averse, indirect communicators, and relationship-oriented.

Nations such as the United States, Germany, England, and Australia are more autonomous, advocate for equality, take calculated risks, communicate directly, and prioritize results over relationships by placing greater emphasis on work.

Of course, lumping all the countries in a continent together as one culture is demonstrably wrong. India is far different than Thailand, Malaysia, and Japan, even though all are in Asia. Likewise, Brazil differs greatly from Mexico, Argentina, and Colombia.

Also, you must dig deeper than newspaper headlines and televised sound bites to understand national cultures and what is truly happening in each country. For instance, expatriates who live in Mexico will attest to the country's thriving economy, culture, and intelligent middle-class workforce. Mexico City has a vibrant international food scene, complemented by artistic, sporting, and business activities on par with any global city. It is not the cesspool of street crimes, drug cartels, and corruption, as depicted in the U.S. media.

The same applies to overseas perspectives of homelessness, gun violence, unsafe cities and schools, racial prejudices, and mentally exhausting workplaces in the U.S. Yes, there is sporadic truth about these afflictions, but they are spread across 50 states and 333 million people. Likewise, America is not one gigantic culture but dozens of regional, local, historical, and new cultures constantly melding together, changing, and amalgamating.

Relevant Cultural Dimensions

Even though cultural norm differences may increase the likelihood that business partnerships will fail, these differences could become the foundation of mutual trust and strong collaborations if managed properly. We have chosen to highlight for you the global cultural dimensions most pertinent to American business culture and which could cause friction for business leaders from other cultures:

Expressive vs. Neutral

Collectivism vs Individualism

Universalistic vs. Particularistic

Polychronic vs. Monochronic Cultures

Time Orientation

Past, Present, and Future

Heart vs. Mind

Peaches and Coconuts

Silence

Space

Equality vs. Hierarchy

Recognition

Risk versus Prudence

A book cover does not necessarily convey the depth or breadth of the content inside the book, even though these are important bits of knowledge! Likewise, the only way to find meaning, beliefs, history, traditions, norms, values, and genuine reasons is to have the courage to step outside one's comfort zone and into the vast ocean of cultural dimensions.

Of course, to understand cultural tendencies, you must start somewhere. Below are some of the cultural dimensions that are critical to know when dealing with American businesspeople.

Expressive vs. Neutral

Americans are not afraid to express themselves. They were raised with this ingrained in their heads from their early school days. When an American talks more than expected and displays emotion, a Japanese person need not be suspicious. Similarly, a Kuwaiti person need not be put off if an American appears less enthusiastic about a project. These are cultural tendencies that can be overcome at the individual level.

The authors of this book have observed that leaders in the United States tend to appreciate international leaders who are transparent and candid. Most Americans find it very difficult to read people when non-verbal clues are absent and not enough written or spoken words are communicated.

America and Europe are worlds of words, while many other countries around the globe are places where non-verbal communication and putting things into context dominate. International leaders who come from cultures with high-context communication styles face an even greater issue when dealing with Americans and American business culture practices.

Collectivism vs. Individualism

Compared to a Japanese, the likelihood of hearing an American talk more about himself than his company is significantly higher. For Japanese people, the pronoun "I" can be just as awkward as the pronoun "we" is for Americans.

Because of this, international leaders from Brazil, Malaysia, and Bahrain should not be insulted by Americans when they hear them sharing their personal and individual accomplishments inside their companies. "The land of the free" is the birthplace of individualism, as each team member's worth reflects their contribution to the team's significance. Being independent thinkers shows how valuable they are to the team.

Americans view independence as a sign of "intelligent" dependency. Being distinct and straightforward in their communication helps the team succeed. Treating Americans as unique individuals will lead to greater success for leaders from other nations and cultures. Non-Americans need to recognize that putting the American individual first before the group does not diminish the significance of the group. Rather, it completes it.

Best practice: It is not arrogant or boastful for an American to talk about himself, his status, accomplishments, or mistakes made. However, it is best to refrain from taking such comments offensively or personally, even though they may not sit well with your cultural background.

Universalistic vs. Particularistic

As previously mentioned, the law supersedes the individual in the United States. As a result, in a universalistic society, the laws are not altered in response to the needs of any one person or company.

The United States holds the top spot in the universalistic cultural dimension, barely below Switzerland. The "what" is far more important than the "who." People you know or who have recommended you for a job are not more significant than what is written on your résumé. Normally, it is what you are capable of doing that gets you the job, not your surname or connection.

Leaders of organizations in nations such as Venezuela, Russia, India, Mexico, and Japan should not be shocked if U.S. companies adhere to the rules and have conservative interpretations of rules, guidelines, and contracts. They find it awkward to break obligations made in contracts without mutual consent and follow-up.

Best practice: It is important to honor commitments and contractual because they are the cornerstones for establishing and preserving relationships with American firms.

Polychronic vs. Monochronic Cultures

In polychronic cultures, boundaries are treated as flexible means of expression. Meeting agendas are not meant to be a rigid set of instructions to be followed but rather a place to start. Even though a meeting in Saudi Arabia may begin with an agenda, only some subjects may be discussed in one sitting. It is possible for agenda topics to be discussed erratically. Why?

Because in polychronic cultures, relationships are more significant than agendas. Those who build agendas need not be controlled by them. On the other hand, American meeting agendas are structured like detailed flow charts, whereas those in Middle Eastern nations may resemble spaghetti dishes.

Best practice: When you observe an American leader in a meeting switching topics before finishing the previous one, exercise patience. This is particularly true if there is a deadlock among the participants in the meeting or if continuing the conversation could upset someone else. There is always time to set up another side meeting, so why not just move on? Why hold the remaining meeting participants captive by relentlessly lecturing them about a particular subject?

Time Orientation

Americans strongly view "time as money." Hence, showing up late for a meeting is considered disrespectful.

But how late is late? Five minutes late is okay as long as you apologize, but more than ten minutes is considered really awful.

That demonstrates how different cultures have different perspectives about time. A friend from the Middle East once told co-author Ali that he would purposefully arrive late for a meeting with a Westerner to gauge the Westerner's response. The friend believes that if a vendor is not patient with him for being late, what treatment would the Westerner give him if his friend is turned into a captive customer?

Middle Easterners gauge a Westerner's sincerity by his patience, while Westerners and Americans gauge a relationship's depth by adherence to punctuality. These polar-opposite viewpoints must be understood and appreciated for partnerships to last. Otherwise, each negative incident leads to the proverbial straw that breaks the camel's back.

Best practice: If you want to be a valued partner of an American company, be prepared and punctual for meetings. If your delay exceeds five minutes, apologize. Keep in mind that three out of four people worldwide arrive late for meetings; if you want to succeed in dealing with Americans, do not be one of those three people.

Past, Present, and Future

Long-established nations usually place a greater emphasis on their historical accomplishments than on more recent ones! These nations often assume that their previous successes signify their excellent present and promising future. "We have done it before. We can do it all over again," they tell themselves.

Conversely, relatively young countries like the United States prioritize the here and now. Because they have not been around for that long, Americans revere their recent triumphs and live in the future.

One phrase that captures American society is, "What have you done for me lately?" Workplace performance reviews are done annually rather than every ten years. Quarterly financial reports are the norm, unlike the five-year financial reports generated in some Asian countries.

Best practice: When attempting to establish a commercial partnership with an American company, mention your most recent achievements in your field. While the past is significant, Americans could be hesitant to do business with foreign companies, particularly small ones, if there is no clear evidence of the company's current state and recent accomplishments. The business world is changing at warp speed, and American leaders want to know that you are either ahead of the curve or at least aligned with the rapid changes happening.

Heart vs. Mind

When making decisions, Americans tend not to be as emotionally invested as many individuals from other nations. Although Americans use both their hearts and minds when making decisions, the mind has a greater influence.

On the other hand, compared to Americans, leaders in England and Germany are generally led even more by their heads than by their feelings.

An American colleague of co-author Ali expressed interest in giving a sales pitch to a German customer before traveling to meet with an Egyptian customer. Since the subject of the presentation was the same, he thought using the same presentation for both made sense. As an American, the colleague believed efficiency was more important than effectiveness.

Would using the same presentation for both customers be acceptable and effective? Definitely not!

The German customer's rational mind would lead them to their decision, while the Egyptian's heart would be the leading factor in their decision-making process. The two customers would both employ their hearts and minds but to different degrees. For each, one side would pull more weight and have greater influence.

Ultimately, neither customer was entirely satisfied because the colleague disregarded the co-author's advice and used the identical slide deck for both presentations. While the Egyptian customer worried that too much information would affect their feelings about the goods being promoted, the German customer requested much more information. The German customer said, "Please give us more information next time to help us make up our minds." Meanwhile, the Egyptian remarked, "Please do not bring anything more than needed lest that might cause us a change of heart."

Adapting to the cultural-driven needs of your audience – whether that is your business partner, customer, or prospect – is essential.

Best practice: Give others the respect they deserve. It will be more effective to combine reasoning and emotions rather than leaning just one way. You may always add more backup slides to your presentations if more material is required. But only overburden them with additional information once specifically requested.

Peaches and Coconuts

Americans have been dubbed the Peach Culture, partially because they are usually receptive to having new individuals in their lives. It is not too difficult to get to know Americans. You can start a discussion and make others laugh to the point that someone watching from the sidelines could assume you have known each other for ages.

Reaching the center of a peach feels just like that. You go quickly at first, but you will soon come to a solid wall. Although it may be complex and challenging, getting to know Americans deeply is possible.

83

Americans are easy to talk to and get to know (on the surface). But different strategies will be needed for each. You might learn about their background and worldviews, but refrain from inquiring about their income, political thinking, or religious views. At that point, the discussion may end abruptly. You will need to spend a lot more time getting to know them if you want to proceed past the surface of the peach seed.

On the other hand, some cultures are known as "coconut cultures." Like coconuts, people from these cultures are soft on the inside but hard on the outside (in terms of relationship building). Obviously, it takes less work to get to the center of a peach than it does for a coconut. The only people who can break through the outer shell of someone from a coconut culture are those who have demonstrated over time that they are reliable and authentic.

Although they are friendlier, more private, and more welcoming than Americans, Japanese people share this aspect with other coconut cultures. But when you spend more time with them, and they get to know you, they open up to you and let you in.

Our perspectives on other cultures are biases that impact cross-cultural communications and partnerships. For example, many Americans believe that Russians and Germans are cold and do not display emotions. In contrast, Russians and Germans may initially believe that Americans are superficial, artificial, and grin without a purpose.

Americans tend to be quite amiable and have big smiles. Get used to smiling more when working with Americans. And remember, these stereotypes have a foundational truth. Still, each person you interact with is a unique individual who will almost definitely have aspects of their character that are not aligned with their cultural heritage, upbringing, or stereotyping.

Silence

Silence is viewed differently across cultures. Long periods of silence during conversations make most Americans uncomfortable. The next time you hold a meeting, conduct an exercise with Americans by asking, "What do you think this year's next disruptive technology will be?" Say it with the intention of providing them with the solution and then observe them.

You will likely receive a response within five seconds. Americans ask questions and often do not wait for an answer before sharing their points of view or providing answers to the questions they ask. Other cultures use rhetorical questions more frequently; sometimes, Americans may view these questions as real questions and not rhetorical ones! That behavior will drive Americans up the wall! Get to the point! Time is money!

Best practice: Americans often finish your sentences for you because they disdain silence. Try not to take it personally!

Space

People from cultures that place a higher value on interpersonal relationships tend to stand closer to one another than Americans. The next time you see two Americans standing and conversing, notice the distance between them. Usually, it is an arm's length away. That is comfortable spacing for Americans. Personal space is different for the further-standing Japanese and the closer-standing Arabs.

Best practice: Refrain from approaching Americans up close and wrapping your arms around them, especially if you plan to do so for longer than two seconds. Additionally, if an American stands at a distance that you find too distant, appears cold, or is off-putting, do not attempt to move closer to them. This is bidirectionally effective. Let them choose the distance!

Equality vs. Hierarchy

How the most powerful members of a society decide the best course of action in response to events and occurrences shapes cultures. It is hard for those used to hierarchy to step beyond their norm and choose the less-traveled path.

On the other hand, Americans are quite at ease ringing the door of their boss's office and addressing them by their first names. Such informal directness makes people uneasy in Saudi Arabia, Mexico, China, India, Japan, Russia, and Italy. However, Americans are usually informal and are not restrained by titles and positions.

Even though progress has been made globally in terms of equality regardless of race, gender, religion, and other characteristics, challenges and disparities still exist in many areas. For instance, female leaders reaching influential executive ranks in America are at the same level as international male leaders. That might create an uncomfortable situation for some international male leaders. But it is something they will have to accept.

An American female leader shared with co-author Ali that a male customer only treated her well once she proved herself intelligent and qualified to discuss company matters. She said that while the customer spoke English well, he would speak in English with her American colleague, who would turn and speak with her in English. Her colleague played the role of an interpreter between two people who spoke English!

Best practice: If you are called by your first name, do not take it personally or feel offended. Americans consider letting go of formality a show of egalitarianism and openness. Another piece of advice would be to abandon the assumption that decisions and high-level leadership positions are limited only to male American leaders.

Recognition

How do people from different cultures acknowledge and motivate one another?

The foundation of American society is individualism. Most people would prefer to receive individual recognition and personal rewards for a job done well. In contrast, people in collectivistic nations like China, Japan, and France would rather not be singled out in front of their teams.

In a collectivistic society, giving individual praise in a one-on-one discussion behind closed doors or acknowledging the team would be more acceptable. That is not the case in America. Not singling out and recognizing a team member in a meeting for a good performance might not rest well with an American who worked above and beyond expectations or produced stellar results.

What is the best way to determine how someone wants to be recognized? The two most effective methods are: 1) find out from other colleagues who know the person well how they have previously preferred to be recognized, or 2) ask the person, in private, the following question: "What method of recognition do you think people prefer to be recognized?" This inquiry frequently yields information about how the person wishes to be treated.

Best practice: Individuals should be treated according to their preferences. Rewarding an American publicly in front of peers or bosses should occur only when you are certain that you are not excluding anyone else and that the American does not adhere to other cultures.

Risk vs. Prudence

Americans enjoy taking calculated chances and making wise selections. "YOLO," or "You Only Live Once," is a phrase you may encounter. This expression, which emphasizes the value of "winging it" or attempting to be comfortable in uncomfortable situations, is primarily used by younger generations.

All American generations share this, albeit to differing degrees. The foundation of America is experimentation and pushing the envelope. This applies equally in social situations and business.

Best practice: Display your spirit of adventure while maintaining a solid foundation in data and facts. As long as innovation is shared with them beforehand and precautions are taken to reduce hazards, Americans are receptively open.

Cultural Agility and Appreciation

The best way to close these cultural dimension gaps is to appreciate other cultures and be culturally agile.

This is not to say you should attempt any form of cultural appropriation. Numerous times, the authors have witnessed non-Americans donning oversized Texas cowboy hats in attempts to fit into American culture. The smiles and laughter they receive are not of respect and gratitude but rather of embarrassment and derision.

Cultural agility and appreciation are two-way streets. It applies to everyone visiting countries outside their own. Here is how co-author Steven explains this to his American audiences.

> I am not a fan of golf. Although I have played golf a few times, I could never dedicate the time to improving my game at the driving range. Also, it is not a sport I would ever watch on TV.
>
> Since I know that golf is extremely important to Japanese businessmen, I have learned how to indulge their interests to build relationships with them.
>
> Before I embark on any trips to Japan, I peruse various golfing websites for a few hours to update myself on the latest happenings in the sport. I also find the results for the last two to three major events.
>
> Hence, in most of my meetings in Japan, I ask the other person their thoughts on these latest golf stories and events. They usually talk for 4-5 minutes, sharing their thoughts or comments as appropriate.
>
> Simply by asking questions about a sport that interests them a lot and listening attentively to their responses, I create a deeper bond with them. I have even had a few people tell others that I am a huge golf fan because of the questions I ask. I never let on that it is not a sport I follow with any deep interest.

Now, some people in my audiences tell me I am being inauthentic. But I am not. I am authentically interested in the relationship and, thus, authentically interested in their views on the topic.

It's like when I visit my mother. She will spend 30-40 minutes telling me the latest about her neighbors, her phone calls with friends, and even her latest Canasta card games. Am I interested in any of these topics? Not really. But she is my mom, and thus, I listen acutely to what interests her. It's the same for developing business relationships across cultures.

The next chapter shares additional tips for success in dealing with American firms and businesspeople.

CHAPTER 5

Your Next Steps for Success

W e encourage you to take advantage of the opportunities driving global and American economic growth. There will be ups and downs, but history shows that those who partner with American businesses usually reap the rewards for doing so.

Initially, this is a sprint race, not a marathon. American businesspeople are focused on short-term wins and rapid results. Planning for long-term relationships is great. Executing a quick-win, immediate profitability strategy is better. The emphasis is on "quick." Always remember: time is money!

Thus, focus early in the relationship on how you can best help your American partners improve their bottom-line profitability through cost reductions, faster time to market, shortened supply chains, reduced exchange rate risks, or higher revenues. In cricket, there is the phrase "get some quick runs on the board." That is your best approach for partnering with American firms – get some quick wins and results that benefit you both.

As we have mentioned several times throughout this book, focus on the business aspects of the relationship first. Yes, this may initially feel uncomfortable, but do not take it personally. Be flexible in your interpretations of how the relationship is initially progressing. However, know that your frustrations will be appreciated and rewarded after the contract is signed and your early wins together are recognized.

Additionally, make every effort to support American companies during difficult times. They will remember you with greater respect and fondness once the storm passes. Co-author Ali recounts how, in a sales executive meeting, someone from the audience questioned whether they should continue exerting effort to sell airplanes to airlines in dire need of money. "The best time to sell to airlines is when their suitcases are empty," responded the head of the sales group.

Observe and Absorb

The cultural dimensions described in Chapter Four (Cross-Cultural Gaps and Bridges) are based on the dominant behaviors and thinking of the majority population in developed and developing countries. But you and your team will not be dealing with the majority of Americans. You will be dealing with a handful of unique individuals and their individualistic behaviors, thinking, beliefs, biases, and preferences.

And, of course, each person you interact with will be impacted – to a lesser or greater degree – by the corporate culture within their workplace environment.

These cultural dimensions are a good starting point for understanding how to partner successfully with Americans. However, true knowledge comes from observing and paying close attention to the individuals you deal with. Few, if any, will adhere 100% to every cultural and social dimension that characterizes the medium of the American cultural spectrum. However, almost all will adhere to standard and conventional American business culture practices, codes, ethics, and conduct.

This is why there is no magical Harry Potter wand to guide your working relationships with American businesspeople. Developing and growing these relationships is an art, not a science. The art of cultural understanding comes through observation and your willingness to be flexible and put aside your cultural preferences and tendencies. This is your best practice for success.

Likewise, to make your team successful, you must share your observations and learnings with everyone on your team. Use these as a starting point for training and discussions of cross-cultural dimensions and how to communicate effectively with your American business partners.

If you Fail to Prepare, Prepare to Fail

Make a sincere assessment of your own prejudices first, then learn about the influences of society and your immediate family and relatives. Is arriving late acceptable in your culture? Understanding the extent to which you and your culture will contribute to the divide between you and Americans may help you prepare more effectively for potential problems.

After self-evaluating your cultural background, including your country's common and accepted business practices, study American culture, including its values, customs, and acceptable and undesirable behaviors.

From this helicopter view of American society and culture, turn your attention to researching the American company's corporate culture. How closely does it adhere to the American national culture? In which other countries has it successfully conducted business? In which other countries has it faced hurdles and obstacles or even withdrawn from?

As an international leader, you will need to start with yourself first by asking the following questions:

- How much has my cultural programming influenced my behavior?

- How much has the influence of my family and relatives influenced me?

- How much have I reacted to these influences that have shaped my mindset?

Only after you ask these questions should you turn your reflection toward your American partner and ask the following:

- Do I know, and does my team know, enough about the true American culture?

- Do I know the regional culture my partner subscribes to (Northwest, Deep South, etc.)

- To what extent does my partner adhere to the national and regional aspects of American culture?

- How much does my partner subscribe to their company's corporate culture?

Additionally, we recommend that you meet with their business partners in other parts of the world. What has worked well? What have been the key issues in partnering with them? What were some of the initial hurdles encountered, and how were these overcome? What other lessons are they willing to share?

With this knowledge of yourself, your organization, and your potential American partner, you may confidently venture into unexplored areas, including the opportunity to do business together.

Take the role of the observer. Listen more than speaking. Watch more and do less until you have a better picture of the identity of the individuals you will work with. The authors of this book provide individual and group mentoring and coaching, both virtually and in-person, that may help you and your team be more effective in your partnership. Please reach out to us if you need anything.

However, be mindful that there is a chance the American you are dealing with only partially embraces mainstream American culture. Gaining trust will unlock the door to fantastic collaborations with American businesses. The willingness to alter your behavior without compromising your own principles is key to a successful partnership.

Advice for success that can help international companies attract American firms are:

- Reputation

- Sharing of American Values

- Adherence to American Working Together principles

- Offer business advantages in terms of costs, schedules, and quality assurance

- Ensure low financial risks, business health, personal safety, and security of international property

- Resiliency and innovation

- Be able to supply what the potential American partner lacks in terms of expertise, skills, and production capacity.

This Is A Team Sport

Be willing to invest in developing the relationship by sending your second-level and operational managers to meet their U.S. counterparts. Success is best built on having multiple layers of people-to-people relationships. While the relationship may start at the C-suite level, it will be fortified at lower leadership and middle management levels.

As co-author Steven often says, "Mid-level leaders and managers are the glue between strategy and execution." You want to ensure that this glue bonds tightly across all levels of both organizations. This is even truer when it comes to cross-border and cross-cultural partnerships.

It is much easier to reconcile differences and overcome personality clashes for people who have met face-to-face than for those whose only connections have been virtual meetings or via email. This is especially important if

English is a second or third language for your team members. The major cause of execution breakdown is often miscommunication and misunderstanding by people who assume they are communicating effectively.

A few thousand dollars in travel expenses early in the partnership may stave off hundreds of thousands of expenses caused by errors, lost productivity, and quality errors later. Not to mention the physical and emotional costs to your staff from cross-cultural conflicts, dramas, and miscommunication.

Be Patient

It is critical that you always remain authentically you. At the same time, successfully crossing the chasm of cultural differences and business practice dissimilarities requires being culturally agile and flexible. Crossing these divides takes time, patience, and practice.

The good news is that effectively and successfully working across boundaries and closing cultural gaps is a skill. Like all skills, it can be enhanced through usage, observation, reflection, effort, and more practice.

One last tip: you can be less culturally flexible when meetings with Americans are held in your home country. On the other hand, it is vital to be more culturally flexible when visiting or meeting with American businesspeople in the U.S.

Almost all cultural differences (both nationalistic and corporate) can be mitigated or overcome through dialog. This is especially true when working with Americans, who typically appreciate direct and honest communication. So, when (not if) a cultural issue arises, be willing to discuss it with your American counterparts openly. And the sooner, the better.

When doing so, ask them for their suggested solutions before proffering yours. This will ensure a more productive conversation focused on solution generation instead of one centered on blaming and shaming.

To successfully partner with people from outside your country and culture, a lifelong learning mindset is advised. Hopefully, you will be continually amazed and grateful for what you learn about other cultures and the business practices of others. As co-author Steven is fond of saying, "Never stop learning for life never stops teaching."

Several decades ago, and before the leaps in communication technology and social media, sharing photos and videos was the only way to see what customers and teammates working in other countries looked like.

One of co-author Ali's American Caucasian colleagues, who worked in the United States, supported an American customer working in Europe for months. However, he never had the chance to see him in person. The American customer had a Caucasian first and last name. He also spoke with a Minnesotan accent. Months passed, and the colleague thought his American customer was white and from Minnesota until he met him in person.

As it turned out, the customer was a second-generation Asian American whose parents immigrated to the Midwest of the United States, where the American customer was born. One can imagine what went through the American Caucasian's head when he saw his customer in person.

America is more diverse than ever. As previously suggested, one should gauge the subscription of American individual to their nation, region, city, ethnic background, and corporate culture. Even then, one may be surprised.

Be an Exemplifier

You can start to become successful in the global business world by utilizing and practicing the techniques and best practices shared throughout this book. Here is your road map:

Respect cultural differences. Avoid thinking that one cultural approach to life is better than another. All have positives and negatives. Respect the culture and business tendencies of those you work and partner with. Most importantly, understand the complexity and nuances of business, corporate, and national cultures.

Build self-awareness in your own cultural predispositions and where you tend to gloss over differences in others. It is critical to understand and work with these differences, not shove them aside, hoping they will autocorrect or meld together over time.

Focus on the desire to work together. There will always be glitches in business and personal relationships. Focus on the overall desire to achieve progress and profitability together. With open communication and a commitment to succeed together, those annoying hiccups can always be overcome or tolerated by each other.

Build trust across cultural boundaries by listening, asking questions, and being attentive to nonverbal signals. Asking questions for clarification and understanding is a best practice, especially when dealing with American businesspeople.

Assumptions often lead to wrong courses of action and costly course corrections.

Be flexible. You do not have to meet each other halfway. However, all parties must be flexible and adaptable when dealing across geographies, cultures, and generations.

Connect at an individual level. Business is done between and by people, not by inanimate corporate entities. Cultural stereotypes are a good place to start your cultural understanding and knowledge, but always remember that you are dealing with individuals and their own set of values, beliefs, customs, wants, desires, and needs. This is particularly true in the highly diverse American culture.

Think twice before responding. Ensure that you fully understand the other person's questions or comments. Before responding, is there a clarification question you can ask to surface more details?

For these reasons, listening more than speaking, observing, and postponing judgment will help you better understand the individuals you interact with. This is a key to enjoying successful partnerships.

And lastly, keep the big picture in mind. As we wrote in the Introduction, as more people work and partner with others outside their core cultures, more people will understand that we are all part of one humanity and that our similarities outweigh our differences.

Thus, as you partner with American firms and their people successfully, you will not only become a more successful international businessperson, but you may also help make the world a more peaceful, kinder, and compassionate place for our children and grandchildren to inherit. Again, for that, we thank you.

Idioms and Acronyms

American

A day late and a dollar short means someone has arrived too late or with insufficient resources to make a difference. The expression originated in the 20th century, reflecting a time when being slightly off in timing or budget could lead to significant consequences, especially in business or finance.

A penny for your thoughts – a phrase used for asking someone what they are thinking, often when they appear lost in thought. Dates back to the 16th century and originates as a British idiom first used by Sir Thomas More in his book *Four Last Things*.

Aunt Sally – someone or something set up as an easy target for criticism in order to deflect it from others. Originating from a traditional British fairground game where a figure called "Aunt Sally" was thrown at with objects, symbolizing someone who is an easy target for attack or ridicule

Back to the drawing board – indicates starting again from scratch when an idea or plan fails. Believed to have originated in the 1940s, when engineers or designers would return to a chalk drawing board after an unsuccessful attempt at solving a problem.

Ballpark figure refers to an approximate estimate or general range. It is often used in budgeting and production forecasting. It originated in the U.S. in the mid-20th century, most likely in the business world, to suggest an estimate that gets you "in the ballpark" or close to the right answer.

Barking up the wrong tree – means to pursue a mistaken or misguided course of action. Originating in 19th-century American frontier culture to describe hunting dogs that barked up the wrong tree and gave their handlers a wrong target.

Bed of nails – refers to uncomfortable, unpleasant, or painful situations. Likely derived from the ancient practice of Hindu ascetics who lay on beds of nails as a form of self-mortification, symbolizing discomfort and hardship.

Bed of roses means an easy or comfortable situation. It is the opposite of a challenging situation. It originated in a 16th-century poem by Christopher Marlowe, in which he describes a pastoral scene that includes a bed of roses.

Behind the eight ball describes someone in a difficult position, particularly one with limited options. The term comes from the game of pool, where being "behind the eight ball" typically means being in a position where a successful shot is difficult or impossible.

Beef up – means to strengthen or increase the size of something, often a report or document with insufficient information or data. Probably derived from the idea that eating beef helps to build strength.

Best thing since sliced bread – refers to something considered extremely innovative or beneficial, suggesting it is the best invention since the convenience of pre-sliced bread. It became popular in the 1920s after commercially available sliced bread was introduced.

Bite off more than you can chew – means to take on more responsibility or tasks than one can handle. Its origin likely comes from biting too much food at once, making it difficult to chew or swallow.

Bite the bullet – implies enduring a painful or difficult situation with courage. Believed to have originated from the practice of wartime soldiers biting down on a bullet to cope with the pain of surgery without anesthesia.

Boil down – means simplifying or summarizing something to its most essential elements. It comes from the process of boiling a liquid to reduce its volume and concentrate its essence (such as simmering pasta sauce).

Boiling the ocean – indicates taking on an overly ambitious or unnecessarily complex task, such as an impractical attempt to boil an entire ocean. The origin of this phrase is unclear, but it is often used in business contexts to describe overreaching goals.

Break a leg – an ironic expression used to wish someone good luck, especially before a performance or business presentation. It is believed to have originated in the theater industry, with various theories advocating the idea of bowing (breaking the leg) or invoking opposite outcomes through superstition.

Burn the candle at both ends refers to someone who is overworking or exerting themselves excessively, often by starting their day early and ending late, thereby depleting their energy. The term originates from the image of burning a candle from both ends simultaneously, thus reducing its lifespan.

Burning the midnight oil – means working late into the night. Likely comes from the historical use of oil lamps for light before electricity.

Circle back – implies returning to a topic or revisiting a conversation at a later time. It is commonly used in business and casual conversations to suggest the need for follow-up.

Close, but no cigar – used when someone almost achieves something but falls slightly short. It probably originated from carnival games where cigars were given as prizes for successful performances.

Couch potato – someone who is extremely sedentary or passive. This implies that the person spends a lot of time watching TV or engaging in similar passive activities. The phrase emerged in the late 20th century to describe a lazy lifestyle.

Curiosity killed the cat – warns against the dangers of unnecessary curiosity or investigation, suggesting that doing so can lead to harm or trouble. Origin uncertain, but likely stems from folklore and literature.

Dirt poor – means being extremely impoverished, with dirt being the metaphor for having almost nothing of value. The term probably originates from the image of people living in houses with dirt floors.

Doesn't pass muster – indicates that something does not meet required standards or expectations and suggests that something that does not pass standards or requirements is unacceptable. It likely originates from the military, where "muster" refers to the inspection of troops.

Don't be a snowflake – advises someone not to be overly sensitive or easily offended. It is a popular term in contemporary culture to describe perceived fragility or overreacting to criticism.

Don't count your chickens before they hatch – advises against assuming success or outcomes before they happen. It uses the imagery of eggs not yet hatched as a metaphor for unpredictable outcomes. It has roots in Aesop's Fables and other early stories.

Don't cry over spilled milk – means not to dwell on small mistakes or things that cannot be undone. Used to emphasize the futility of worrying about things beyond one's control. Likely originated from early folk wisdom.

Drinking the Kool-Aid – implies unthinkingly or mindlessly following or adopting a belief or ideology without questioning it. The origin is linked to the tragic Jonestown incident in 1978, where followers of a cult drank poisoned Kool-Aid.

Drop in the bucket – describes something insignificant compared to the whole, like a single drop into a large bucket of water. It implies how insignificant a single drop can be in a larger context. The term has biblical roots and is referenced in the Book of Isaiah.

Ducks in a row – means to be well-organized or prepared. It likely originates from the natural tendency of ducklings to line up behind their mother, indicating orderly behavior.

Eager beaver – someone who is extremely enthusiastic or industrious, often to an excessive degree. Comes from the reputation of the beaver being a hard-working animal known for its industrious dam-building.

Elephant in the room – refers to an obvious issue or problem that everyone is aware of but nobody wants to face or discuss. It comes from the absurdity of ignoring something as large and conspicuous as an elephant in a confined space.

Fallen through the cracks – something or someone overlooked, neglected, or forgotten. It evokes the image of something slipping through small gaps in wood floors or something/someone escaping attention or care.

Fire away implies speaking or asking questions without hesitation, no matter the social or business circumstances. It likely has military origins, where officers would shout "fire" to command shooting or launching.

Getting something down pat – means mastering a skill or routine to the point where it has become effortless. The term probably comes from the concept of "pat" as something precise, such as a pre-learned response or action.

Get up on the wrong side of the bed – describes someone in a bad mood or with a negative attitude from the start of the day. Likely comes from an old superstition that getting out of the left side of the bed is unlucky.

Go Dutch – means to split the cost of something, usually a meal, among two or more participating people. The origin is unclear, but it is thought to relate to the stereotype of Dutch people being frugal or careful with money.

Going bananas – describes someone who is extremely excited or irrationally enthusiastic. The origin is uncertain but probably refers to the erratic behavior often seen in monkeys.

Going cold turkey – means quitting something suddenly and completely. Typically used to describe stopping a bad habit like smoking, excessive drinking, or drug usage. The origin is unknown but may refer to the physical effects of withdrawal, such as goosebumps resembling turkey skin.

Going the full nine yards – connotes giving your all or doing something thoroughly. The exact origin is unknown, but a common theory suggests it comes from the military, where the full length of a fighter plane's machine gun's ammunition belt is nine yards.

Good Time Charley/Charlie – one devoted to the pursuit of convivial fun and amusement, often without considering responsibilities. This idiom from the early 20th century uses "Charlie," a common name, to depict a carefree individual who prioritizes enjoyment and social activities over more serious pursuits.

Herding cats – describes an attempt to control or coordinate a chaotic situation featuring highly independent elements. Plays on the impossibility of organizing animals as unruly and independent as cats.

Hit the sack – implies going to bed to sleep. It likely originates from the days when beds were filled with sacks of straw, suggesting hitting or lying down on them to sleep.

Hot potato – refers to a sensitive or controversial issue that people prefer to avoid. It likely comes from the discomfort of holding a hot potato and the desire to pass it on quickly.

It's all downhill from here – indicates that things will become easier or less challenging from this point forward.

Alternatively, it can also imply a decline, as in downhill movement, suggesting a drop in quality or stability. Thus, the context surrounding this phrase is critical.

It's a piece of cake – something that is very easy or simple to do. Probably originated with the idea that eating a piece of cake is a straightforward and enjoyable task.

It's for the birds – describes something as worthless or of no value. The origin may come from the notion that some pieces of food are so small and insignificant that they are only suitable for birds to pick at.

It's not rocket science – often used humorously to indicate that something is not complex or difficult to understand. Connotes that something is the opposite of the complexity and challenges associated with learning or understanding rocket science or aerospace engineering.

Jump on the bandwagon – means joining a popular trend or activity because it is gaining momentum or social acceptance. The origin comes from people hopping onto bandwagons during parades or public events.

Jumping the gun – implies acting prematurely or starting something too soon. It likely comes from foot races, where firing the starting gun indicates when to begin. Thus, it suggests starting before a given signal.

Let the cat out of the bag – means to reveal a secret or divulge something meant to remain hidden. It likely originated from old market tricks in which a cat was substituted for a pig in a bag, with the fraud only revealed when the bag was opened.

Let's car park this (or that's a parking lot item) – means setting aside a topic or issue for later discussion. It likely comes from "parking" an idea, suggesting placing it in a figurative parking lot for future consideration.

Losing your touch – means to lose proficiency or expertise in something one was once good at. It suggests someone has lost the magic or finesse associated with a skill or specific activity.

Monday morning quarterback – refers to someone who critiques or judges an event, action, or decision after it has happened, with the benefit of hindsight. It comes from people who analyze and discuss American football games on Monday mornings and offer advice or opinions on what the players or coaches should have done.

More holes than Swiss cheese – describes something with many flaws, inconsistencies, or weaknesses. A metaphor for something not solid or containing many gaps. Based on the imagery of a kind of Swiss cheese known for its many holes.

Move the needle – means to make a noticeable impact or significant change. Likely originates from analog measuring instruments where a needle indicates a change or movement in values.

Nervous Nelly/Nellie – one who is unusually nervous, timid, anxious, or fearful. The term likely originated in the early 20th century in the United States, using "Nelly," a common name, to personify someone who is overly worried or timid.

Nosebleed section – refers to the highest and farthest seats in a venue, such as a concert hall or sports arena. It suggests that the seats are so high that they could cause nosebleeds due to the altitude. Humorously emphasizes the distant perspective and potentially poor view from such seats (or people far removed from a situation).

Not resting/sitting on our laurels – means not relying on past successes and continuing to strive for more. It comes from the ancient tradition of awarding laurel wreaths for achievement, suggesting that resting on them implies complacency.

On the same page -- agreeing or sharing the same understanding or perspective about something. Indicates that both (or all) parties are following the same line of thought. Comes from the imagery of reading from the same page in a book.

Out of pocket – has two meanings: 1) being unavailable or out of reach, and 2) referring to personal expenses incurred that are not reimbursed (usually by one's employer). The second usage originates from paying for something directly from one's pocket or wallet.

Over the moon – describes being extremely happy, delighted, or elated. Its origin probably comes from old English nursery rhymes, such as *Hey Diddle Diddle,* where a cow jumps over the moon.

Passed with flying colors -- means to succeed with distinction or to achieve a task with great success. Likely comes from naval warfare, where ships proudly flew their colors or flags when they returned victorious to their home port.

Pick a bone with someone (or a bone to pick with someone) – means to have a grievance or unresolved issue to discuss or confront with another person. Probably originates from the image of dogs fighting over a bone, indicating conflict or disagreement.

Pie in the sky – describes a hope or dream that is unrealistic or unlikely to be achieved. Attributed to labor activist Joe Hill, who used it in a satirical context, pointing out the folly of empty promises.

Plead the fifth – means to invoke the Fifth Amendment of the U.S. Constitution, which allows individuals to refuse to answer questions that might incriminate them. Used in business and social settings where people do not want to implicate themselves in wrongdoing or making a mistake.

Plugging away – describes persistently working on something, often with steady, continuous effort. Used to emphasize consistency and perseverance by someone.

Put up your dukes – is a call to prepare for a physical fight or confrontation, with "dukes" being a slang term for fists. Possibly derived from 'Duke of York," rhyming slang for fork, a slang term for hand.

Reading between the lines – means understanding a deeper or hidden meaning in a text, statement, or situation. Implies that the true message is not explicitly stated but is implied through context or subtle clues.

Ride shotgun – means to sit in the front passenger seat of a vehicle. Originates from the Wild West period of American history, where a person armed with a shotgun would sit beside a stagecoach driver to protect against bandits.

Right as rain – means to be completely correct or in perfect condition. While the phrase's origin is unclear, it may refer to the predictability of rain to restore balance to the environment.

Run it up the flagpole – means to test or propose an idea to see how it is received or to gauge interest. It likely comes from raising a flag on a flagpole to see if it garners attention or support.

Run the gamut – indicates covering a wide range or extent, often from one end to another. It originates from music terminology, where gamut refers to the full scale of notes.

Run the gauntlet – means to endure a challenging or harrowing series of events. It comes from a military punishment in which a person had to run between two lines of soldiers who would strike them with sticks or other weapons.

Shoot for the moon – means to aim for a high or ambitious goal, even if it seems difficult to achieve. Often used to encourage bold aspirations. Based on the imagery of aiming at something as distant and lofty as the mood.

Silver lining (every cloud has a silver lining) – suggests that even difficult or adverse situations may have a positive aspect. It indicates hope or opportunity, even within a gloomy situation. This phrase likely originates from the imagery of dark clouds with bright edges.

Slim chance – indicates a low probability or unlikely outcome. In this case, "slim" suggests narrowness or smallness, implying that the chance is quite minimal.

Solving world hunger – indicates taking on an overly ambitious or unnecessarily complex task, such as an impractical attempt to boil an entire ocean. The origin of this phrase is unclear, but it is often used in business contexts to describe overreaching goals.

Spill the beans – means to reveal a secret or disclose confidential information. The origin is uncertain but may derive from voting practices in ancient Greece, where beans were used to cast votes, and spilling them could reveal the results prematurely.

Stab someone in the back – means to betray someone who trusted you, implying both deceit and disloyalty. Evokes the treacherous act of attacking someone from behind.

Step up to the plate – means taking responsibility or accepting a challenge. It comes from baseball, where batters step up to the plate to face thrown pitches.

Swing for the fences – means attempting something with great ambition, often hoping to achieve a significant result. Originates from baseball, where batters swing with enough force to drive the ball over the outfield fence for a "home run."

Table an item – means to postpone a discussion or decision on a topic, usually in a meeting or negotiation. It originates from parliamentary procedure where "tabling" means putting something aside for later consideration.

Taste of your own medicine means to experience the same unpleasant treatment or behavior you have inflicted on others. It likely originates from fables or stories where someone gets a "taste" of their own harmful or unpleasant actions.

The ball is in your court – indicating it is someone else's turn to take action or make a decision. It indicates whose responsibility it is to respond or make the next move. Originates from sports like tennis, where the ball moves between players.

Throwing someone under the bus – means sacrificing or blaming someone else to save oneself or to avoid responsibility. It gained popularity in business and politics in the late 20th century. The origin is unclear, but it likely evokes the dramatic imagery of pushing someone into danger or peril to protect oneself or shift blame.

Throwing the baby out with the bathwater – refers to accidentally getting rid of something valuable while discarding something unwanted. The expression probably comes from a time when families shared bathwater and the risk of unintentionally throwing out the baby while emptying the bath.

To be down for something – means to be interested in or willing to participate in something. It is commonly used in informal settings, implying readiness or agreement to join an activity or event.

To be up for something – means to be enthusiastic or willing to engage in an activity or task, similar to the previous idiom "to be down for something."

Too many cooks in the kitchen – indicates too many people involved in a task, leading to chaos or inefficiency. This term likely originated from commercial kitchens, where having multiple cooks can lead to confusion and disorganization.

Twist someone's arm – a metaphorical expression meaning to pressure or coerce someone into doing something against their will. It comes from the imagery of a physical action to force someone into submission.

Up your game – means improving your performance or increasing your effort level. It indicates the need for someone to raise standards. Commonly used in competitive or performance-driven business contexts.

We've got it down pat – means having something fully understood or perfected through practice. It suggests confidence and fluency with a particular skill or task.

When pigs fly – describes something highly unlikely or impossible. It emphasizes the extreme unlikelihood of a given event or outcome and humorously evokes the absurdity of pigs flying.

White on rice – means to be extremely close or inseparable from something or someone. It is often used to describe persistence or close attention to a person or task. The imagery suggests how white rice grains are consistently white, indicating an inherent or tight bond.

English Words and Phrases

Ankle-biters – a colloquial term referring to young children, especially those who are very active or mischievous. It evokes the image of very small toddlers who cling to or nip at an adult's ankles.

Bairn – a word primarily used in Scottish and Northern English dialects to refer to a child. It is derived from the Old English word "beran," which means child or descendant.

Chin wag – an informal chat or conversation. It is likely derived from the image of a person's chin moving up and down while talking, resembling a "wag."

Chuffed – extremely pleased or delighted. Symbolizes a feeling of pride or satisfaction. Thought to derive from dialectal words meaning "swollen with fat" or "puffed up."

Codswallop – nonsense or rubbish. The origin is unclear, but one theory links it to "wallop," a term for beer combined with "cods," possibly signifying imitation or fraudulent.

117

Collywobbles – a feeling of nervousness or an upset stomach. Likely derives from "colic" and "wobbles," suggesting internal discomfort or queasiness.

Doddle – something that is easy to do. Suggests simplicity. Probably derived from the dialect term "daddle," meaning "to walk slowly or aimlessly."

Dog's breakfast (or dog's dinner) – a messy, disorderly, or chaotic situation. It describes situations or tasks that have been poorly organized or are in a state of confusion. The term stems from the notion of how a dog's food bowl is often a jumbled mess.

Donkey's years – a very long time. A play on the phrase "donkey's ears," which are long, leading to a similar-sounding phrase that connotes a lengthy period.

Dropped a clanger – make a noticeable or embarrassing mistake, especially in describing another person incorrectly or inappropriately. Based on the meaning of "clanger," a loud, resonant sound, thus suggesting the error produces a significant noise or impact.

Gormless – lacking intelligence or common sense. It also connotes being foolish. The word comes from "gome" or "gorm," an old word meaning sense or understanding.

Hit it for six – achieving an outstanding success or completely surpassing expectations. The phrase comes from the sport of cricket, where hitting a ball for six runs is an impressive feat.

Hole in the wall – a small, inconspicuous place. It often describes a hidden gem for food or drinks. Also, a slang term for an ATM. The expression evokes the image of a small opening in a wall, suggesting a hidden or secretive location.

It's brass monkeys out – a shortened form of "cold enough to freeze the brass monkeys." Used to express that it is extremely cold outside. The phrase possibly originates from the brass fittings on old naval ships contracting in extreme cold.

Knackered – extremely tired or exhausted. The word is derived from "knacker," a term used for someone who slaughters worn-out horses, suggesting something or someone worn out beyond use.

Know your onions – to be very knowledgeable or skilled in a particular subject. Origins are uncertain, but possibly from the name of British lexicographer C.T. Onions.

Let's get together soon / meet up soon – is a casual invitation to meet or socialize, often said without authenticity or the intent to follow up. It is a common and casual way to close a conversation politely, similar to the U.S. phrase "have a nice day."

Minted – wealthy or rich, suggesting that someone has abundant wealth.

Naff – unstylish, tacky, or in poor taste. Derived from British slang in the 1960s, where naff indicated something unappealing or of low quality.

Table an item—means to discuss a topic more deeply, usually in a meeting or negotiation (opposite meaning for Americans, see above). Originates from a parliamentary procedure where "tabling" means not leaving the table until a resolution is reached.

Tosh – nonsense or rubbish. Derived from British slang, possibly from a word meaning "trash" or "refuse."

Wally – a foolish, inept, or bumbling person.

Yonks – a long period of time.

Acronyms Common in U.S. Businesses

Here is a list of the 50 most common acronyms in U.S. business, along with their definitions, in alphabetical order:

AI - Artificial Intelligence

AOP - Annual Operating Plan

ASAP – As Soon As Possible

API - Application Programming Interface

B2B - Business-to-Business

B2C - Business-to-Consumer

BPM - Business Process Management

BPO - Business Process Outsourcing

BRD - Business Requirements Document

BYOD - Bring Your Own Device

CAPEX - Capital Expenditure

COB – Close of Business

CFO - Chief Financial Officer

CHRO – Chief Human Resources Officer

CIO - Chief Information Officer

CMO - Chief Marketing Officer

COO - Chief Operating Officer

CPA - Certified Public Accountant

CPO – Chief People Officer

CRM - Customer Relationship Management

CRO – Chief Revenue Officer

CSR - Corporate Social Responsibility

CTO - Chief Technology Officer

CYA - Cover Your Assets (or a similar word)

DBA - Doing Business As

D&I - Diversity and Inclusion

EBITDA - Earnings Before Interest, Taxes, Depreciation, and Amortization

EOD - End of Day

EOR – Employer of Record

ERP - Enterprise Resource Planning

ETA – Estimated Time of Arrival

ETL - Extract, Transform, Load

FAQ - Frequently Asked Questions

FTE - Full-Time Equivalent

FWIW – For What It's Worth

HR - Human Resources

IT - Information Technology

KPI - Key Performance Indicator

M&A - Mergers and Acquisitions

MBA - Master of Business Administration

MVP - Minimum Viable Product

NA – Not Applicable

NLT – No Later Than

OKR - Objectives and Key Results

OSHA - Occupational Safety and Health Administration

P&L - Profit and Loss

PMO - Project Management Office

PMP - Project Management Professional

PTO – Paid Time Off

QA - Quality Assurance

R&D - Research and Development

RFI - Request for Information

RFP - Request for Proposal

ROI - Return on Investment

RRR – Reduce, reuse, recycle

RTO – Return To Office

SaaS - Software as a Service

SEO - Search Engine Optimization

SLA - Service Level Agreement

SME - Subject Matter Expert

SOP - Standard Operating Procedure

SWOT - Strengths, Weaknesses, Opportunities, Threats

TBA – To Be Advised

TBD – To Be Determined

TGIF – Thank Goodness It's Friday

TLDR – Too Long, Didn't Read

TMI – Too Much Information

VPN - Virtual Private Network

VTO – Volunteering Time Off

About the Authors

Ali Shami is the CEO and founder of FTD Global, which provides training in cultural sensitivity and leadership. He has worked with worldwide clients, partners, and suppliers for over 30 years. During his extensive tenure as a senior leader at Boeing, he was at the forefront of assisting the aircraft company in marketing its products and services across multiple nations and markets.

Ali led teams in Operations, Customer Service, Customer Engineering, Sales & Marketing, Manufacturing, Product Development, Supplier Management, and Global Engineering. He also provided on-site leadership support to airline customers in Korea, Italy, and England.

Ali received multiple Diversity Awards and was listed among the top 100 Boeing managers who obtained the highest scores in the 2009 employee and business survey.

In addition to his interest in Mentoring, Leadership Training, Technical Research, and writing, he is a public speaker and musician. He has several publications in the technical and leadership fields. Ali produced the first audio material that introduces the Lebanese dialect, which is spoken in the streets of Beirut.

"One Perspective to Creating a Great Team is like one Food Ingredient to Making a Perfect Cuisine!"

Contact Details

E: alishami@FTDGlobal.com

M: +1-425-791-9920

W: www.ftdglobal.com

LinkedIn: https://www.linkedin.com/in/alihshami/

Steven Howard is the award-winning author of 22 leadership, business, and professional development books. In awarding his book *Humony Leadership: Mindsets, Skills, and Behaviors for Being a Successful People-Centric Leader* a Gold Medal, the Nonfiction Authors Association called *Humony Leadership* "a significant work with an important mission."

Humony is a word created by Steven comprising Human, Humanity, and Harmony to emphasize the leading of people and the need for leaders to create workplaces of wellbeing and harmony. He is also the co-author of *Strong Women Speak on Leadership, Success, and Living Well.*

Steven was named one of the 2023 Top 200 Global Biggest Voices in Leadership in recognition of his thought-provoking and leading-edge thinking on leadership. He was also named to the 2023 CREA List of Top Influential Leaders for his thought leadership and writing.

Steven has over 40 years of international senior sales, marketing, and leadership experience. His corporate career covered a wide variety of fields and experiences, including Regional Marketing Director for Texas Instruments Asia-Pacific, Regional Director (South Asian & ASEAN) for TIME Magazine, Global Account Director at BBDO Advertising, handling an international airline account, and Vice President Marketing for Citibank's Consumer Banking Group.

Steven is well-known and recognized for his international and multicultural perspective, having lived in the USA for over 30 years, in Singapore for 21 years, and in Australia for 12 years. He currently resides in Mexico City.

Contact Details

E: steven@CalienteLeadership.com

M: +1-760-835-7870

W: www.CalienteLeadership.com

LinkedIn: https://www.linkedin.com/in/stevenbhoward/

C: https://calendly.com/stevenhoward

Made in the USA
Columbia, SC
09 February 2025

53555800R00074